CALDWELL COLLEGE LIBRARY
CALDWELL, NEW JERSEY

From the Library
of

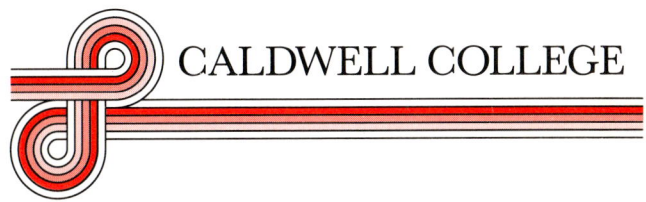

CALDWELL COLLEGE

Caldwell, New Jersey 07006

FOUNDATIONS OF MODERN ECONOMICS SERIES

Otto Eckstein, *Editor*

NEW VOLUMES

Prices and Markets, *Robert Dorfman*
Labor Economics, *John T. Dunlop*
Evolution of Modern Economics, *Richard T. Gill*
Economic Systems, *Gregory Grossman*
Managerial Economics, *John R. Meyer* and *Donald E. Farrar*

SECOND EDITIONS

American Industry: Structure, Conduct, Performance, *Richard Caves*
Money and Credit: Impact and Control, *James S. Duesenberry*
Public Finance, *Otto Eckstein*
Economic Development: Past and Present, *Richard T. Gill*
International Economics, *Peter B. Kenen*
National Income Analysis, *Charles L. Schultze*
Student Guide and Workbook for the Foundations of Modern Economics Series, *R. Hartman* and *E. Gustafson*
Workbook for the Foundations of Modern Economics, *R. Hartman* and *E. Gustafson*

FIRST EDITION

The Price System, *Robert Dorfman*

FOUNDATIONS OF MODERN ECONOMICS SERIES

DONALD E. FARRAR / *Yale University and National Bureau of Economic Research*
JOHN R. MEYER / *Columbia University and Securities Exchange Commission*

Managerial Economics

PRENTICE-HALL, INC. *Englewood Cliffs, New Jersey*

© Copyright 1970 by PRENTICE-HALL, INC., Englewood Cliffs, New Jersey.

All rights reserved. No part of this book may be reproduced
in any form or by any other means without permission
in writing from the publishers. Printed in the United States of America.

P-13-549980-1   C-13-549998-4

Library of Congress Catalog Card No. 73-100106

Designed by Harry Rinehart.

PRENTICE-HALL FOUNDATIONS
OF MODERN ECONOMICS SERIES

Otto Eckstein, *Editor*

Current printing (last digit):
10 9 8 7 6 5 4 3 2 1

PRENTICE-HALL INTERNATIONAL, INC., *London*
PRENTICE-HALL OF AUSTRALIA, PTY., LTD., *Sydney*
PRENTICE-HALL OF CANADA, LTD., *Toronto*
PRENTICE-HALL OF INDIA, PVT. LTD., *New Delhi*
PRENTICE-HALL OF JAPAN, INC., *Tokyo*

Foundations

of Modern Economics Series

Economics has grown so rapidly in recent years, it has increased so much in scope and depth, and the new dominance of the empirical approach has so transformed its character, that no one book can do it justice today. To fill this need, the Foundations of Modern Economics Series was conceived. The Series, brief books written by leading specialists, reflects the structure, content, and key scientific and policy issues of each field. Used in combination, the Series provides the material for the basic one-year college course. The analytical core of economics is presented in *Prices and Markets* and *National Income Analysis,* which are basic to the various fields of application. *Prices and Markets* takes the beginning student through the elements of that subject step-by-step. *The Price System* is a more sophisticated alternative carried over from the first edition. Two books in the Series, *The Evolution of Modern Economics* and *Economic Development: Past and Present,* can be read without prerequisite and can serve as an introduction to the subject. In this edition, two new books appear in the Series, *Managerial Economics* and *Labor Economics*. This completes the initial design of the Series.

The Foundations approach enables an instructor to devise his own course curriculum rather than to follow the format of the traditional textbook. Once analytical principles have been mastered, many sequences of topics can be arranged and specific areas can be explored at length. An instructor not interested in a complete survey course can omit some books and concentrate on a detailed study of a few fields. One-semester courses stressing either macro- or micro-economics can be readily devised. The instructors guide to the Series indicates the variety of ways the books in the Series can be used.

This Series is an experiment in teaching. The positive response to the first edition has encouraged us to continue, and to develop and improve, the approach. The thoughtful reactions of many teachers who have used the books in the past have been of immense help in preparing the second edition —in improving the integration of the Series, in smoothing some rough spots in exposition, and in suggesting additional topics for coverage.

The books do not offer settled conclusions. They introduce the central problems of each field and indicate how economic analysis enables the reader to think more intelligently about them, to make him a more thoughtful citizen, and to encourage him to pursue the subject further.

Otto Eckstein, *Editor*

Contents

One   **THE MANAGERIAL FUNCTION**   1

Objectives. Information Sources: Basic Financial Data. Conclusion.

Two   **MARGINAL ANALYSIS**   9

Basic Concepts. Basic Price and Output Decisions. Multiple Markets, Price Discrimination and Government Regulation. The Inventory Lot Size Problem. Conclusion.

Three   **MATHEMATICAL PROGRAMMING**   23

Mathematical Programming and the Operations Research Approach. Linear Programming: An Illustrative Example. Mathematical Programming and the Derivation of Shadow Prices. Process Formulations of Mathematical Programming. Generalizations and Further Applications.

Four   **CAPITAL BUDGETING**   47

The Present Value Criterion. Alternative Criteria. Some Complications: Multiple Period Planning and Budget Constraints. Sources and Users of Funds and the Cost of Capital.

Five   **UNCERTAINTY**   68

The Need for Analysis of Uncertainty. An Illustrative Example: Wildcatting for Oil. Valuation by Certainty Equivalence. Valuation by Expected Values. Risk Preference and Valuation. Evaluation of Strategies.

Six   **POSTSCRIPT**   101

SELECTED READINGS   105

APPENDIX   107

INDEX   111

Managerial Economics

The Managerial Function

CHAPTER ONE

OBJECTIVES

The study of managerial economics begins with developing an awareness of the environment within which managerial decisions take place. It is a complex environment. Considerable disagreement exists, for example, as to what managerial goals should even be.[1] In large measure this disagreement reflects the fact that management serves a great many diverse interests: those of stockholders, employees, the local community, the larger society or nation within which the firm operates and finally, of course, the interests of specific members of the management group itself. Furthermore, management can be a highly diverse group; new

---

Both authors would like to acknowledge at the outset that this book is a joint effort in its entirety and disclaim any specific divisions of responsibility regarding its several chapters. In this vein, the order of authorship is alphabetical and carries no implication of leadership or seniority. The authors also wish to acknowledge Professor Richard S. Bower, who reviewed the original manuscript, and thank him for his many helpful suggestions.

[1] A long controversial literature exists on the nature of managerial goals. Among others, see: W. J. Baumol, *Business Behavior, Value, and Growth* (New York: The Macmillan Company, 1959); A. Berle, "The Impact of the Corporation on Classical Economic Theory," *The Quarterly Journal of Economics,* Vol. 79, No. 1 (February 1965); A. Berle and G. Means, *The Modern Corporation and Private Property* (New York: The Macmillan Company, 1932); R. M. Cyert and J. G. March, *A Behavioral Theory of the Firm* (Englewood Cliffs, N.J.: Prentice-Hall, Inc., 1963); C. Kaysen, "Another View of Corporate Capitalism," *The Quarterly Journal of Economics,* Vol. 79, No. 1 (February 1965); F. Machlup, "Theories of the Firm: Marginalist, Behavioral, Managerial," *The American Economic Review,* Vol. 62, No. 1 (March 1967); R. Marris, *The Economic Theory of Managerial Capitalism* (New York: Free Press of Glencoe, 1964); E. Penrose, *The Theory of the Growth of the Firm* (Oxford: Blackwell, 1959); S. Peterson, "Corporate Control and Capitalism," *The Quarterly Journal of Economics,* Vol. 79, No. 1 (February 1965); O. Williamson, *The Economics of Discretionary Behavior: Managerial Objectives in the Theory of the Firm* (Englewood Cliffs, N.J.: Prentice-Hall, Inc., 1964).

managerial trainees may view the firm very differently from middle level executives, who, in turn, may have different perspectives than top level management.

Ask an executive to define his goals for the firm and a whole set of partially contradictory answers may well be forthcoming. He might, for example, cite alternatively the maximization of profits, or sales or the value of the firm's assets as his goals; in addition, he might discuss stability of employment, managerial control, employee and community welfare, customer satisfaction, or the minimization of costs. Difficulty in defining goals is not limited to businessmen, however. Bentham's "greatest good for the greatest number" satisfied countless generations of intellectuals before someone finally realized that it contained one "greatest" too many. Moreover, businessmen may be well aware that their proclaimed goals are less than fully, or even comfortably, compatible with one another. Quite properly, they feel often that one of management's key responsibilities is reconciling or arbitrating divergent views and interests. Consequently, managers, like politicians, may think of their objectives in terms of service to, or tradeoffs between, diverse and sometimes bitterly competitive interests and interested parties.

The absence of a single well-defined objective usually creates analytical problems when a decision is being made. Actions that are rational in terms of one objective (maximizing profits, for example) may be largely inconsistent with another goal (such as maximizing employee welfare). All of this suggests that conflicts are almost bound to arise in the situations modern managers confront. These conflicts must be reconciled somehow—and quite often at the highest levels of management. But no general solution or resolution is now at hand. It is important to recognize, however, that conflicts exist and must be dealt with, for analysis, or choice, presupposes criteria or goals.

Within these pages, we will largely "beg the question" of conflict and conflict resolution. We shall simply assume that managerial goals or objectives can be specified. Indeed, we shall go even further and assume in most instances that a firm's primary goal is *profit maximization,* or maximization of the present value of the firm's expected future earnings. We shall define these terms more precisely in subsequent chapters. At this point, a rough translation for such a statement is that a firm's primary objective is to maximize the firm's market value to its owners. We would not want to defend this assumption to the death. But we can point out that managerial economics is built largely on the presumption that profit maximization is the dominant goal of management. And even if it is not, the analytical techniques built on that assumption can still be very helpful in analyzing certain limited problems. In the chapters that follow we will point out a few of these limitations—but only a few —so the student should remember that these techniques have definite limitations.

To satisfy his firm's goals, however these may be specified, a business manager today has at his disposal certain resources in the form of people and capital (plant and equipment and money to finance his operations).

He also has available a growing body of knowledge regarding utilization of these resources to meet objectives. Basically, this book treats some of the particular analytical tools that make up this body of administrative or managerial knowledge. However, to apply any analytical techniques one needs information. So before discussing the analytical techniques themselves, let us survey a few of the more basic data generated by and available to business managers, specifically those summarizing the financial position and achievements of the firm.

INFORMATION SOURCES: BASIC FINANCIAL DATA

Management clearly requires information. But information requirements range widely: they include external reports to owners, creditors and governments (for taxes, social security plans and so forth); they also include internal reports for control, forecasting and decision purposes. Among the most important external reports rendered by managers are those that provide financial information to owners and creditors. Financial information can be used for comparison purposes, cutting across functional boundaries within a firm and, to a lesser extent, between firms; thus it can be useful in some instances for planning, controlling and motivating future activities, as well as for evaluating past performance.

Financial reports come in four primary packages: (1) balance sheets; (2) income statements; (3) funds flow analyses; and (4) ratio analyses. Each will be developed and discussed briefly below. Basic differences in purpose, structure and information conveyed by these and less formal types of documents can be illustrated by an example.

Suppose a young man sets out to establish a new enterprise; call it the Alpha Corporation. We could dream up an exciting product for him to manufacture, but it is quite unnecessary for our purposes. Let us suppose simply that by December 31 of 1965 our entrepreneur has scraped together $15,000 in funds from his own resources and has obtained a $20,000 bank loan, the principal to be repaid in four annual installments of $5,000 each. Let's further assume that by this date he has invested these funds in $25,000 worth of fixed assets, $8,000 of inventories, and holds $2,000 in cash. Should one take a snapshot of the firm's financial condition at this point in time, summarizing as succinctly as possible what it *owns* and what it *owes*, the resulting document would be called a balance sheet; it would be organized roughly as shown in Table 1-1.

Balance Sheet

Several basic characteristics of the balance sheet can be highlighted by even a very brief examination. The first, as suggested earlier, is that a balance sheet *freezes* the firm's financial condition at a single instant in time.

It summarizes *stocks*, or *levels*, of assets and liabilities; it tells us nothing about how effectively these are applied to produce *flows* of funds or profits over an interval of time. A second point to emphasize is that entries on a balance sheet do in fact "balance," in the sense that total assets, by definition, are equal to total liabilities and net worth—where net worth, the balancing item, is that portion of the firm's assets provided by its owners; or, conversely, that portion *not* funded by outside creditors. A third point to be noted is that both assets and liabilities are further divided into current (short term) and noncurrent (long term) maturity classes. The former includes relatively liquid items such as cash, inventories and debt payable within a year; the latter picks up less liquid items such as land, plant and equipment, and debt whose maturity is more than one year away.

Table 1-1 CONSOLIDATED BALANCE SHEET, "ALPHA CORPORATION"

December 31, 1965

Assets—at Cost		Liabilities and Net Worth	
Current Assets		Current liabilities	
Cash	$2,000	Debt (to bank)	$ 5,000
Inventories	8,000	Noncurrent liabilities	
		Debt (to bank)	15,000
Total current assets	10,000	Total liabilities	20,000
Fixed assets			
Plant & equipment	15,000	Net worth	15,000
Land	10,000		
Total noncurrent assets	25,000		
Total assets	$35,000	Total liabilities and net worth	$35,000

Any number of parties—owners, security analysts, creditors, etc.—may be interested in the financial condition summarized by a firm's balance sheet. Indeed, with attention mainly focused on the relative size and maturity structure of assets and liabilities, balance sheets are designed largely with actual or potential creditors in mind. By analyzing our young man's balance sheet, for example, his banker can see at a glance that although the firm's ability to cover near term obligations may be relatively secure (depending on the marketability of the firm's inventories), as $10,000 of liquid assets are held against $5,000 in short term liabilities, its overall debt position is relatively high, for more than half the firm's total assets are debt financed. In the absence of favorable operating results, then, creditors may have some difficulty recovering their capital from sale of the firm's assets alone. These, basically, are the types of questions balance sheets are designed to help answer.

Income Statement

The income statement is a second type of financial statement and has quite a different orientation from the balance sheet. The income statement will be of special interest to our young owner. Let us assume that following the first full year of his firm's operation, our entrepreneur observes with some satisfaction that from sales of $100,000, he has been able to extract a gross cash flow (after paying for labor and materials) of $12,500. Some of these funds must be diverted to pay $1,000 in interest charges (at 5 percent on the firm's $20,000 bank loan), and some must go for taxes. Both represent direct cash flows from the firm to outside claimants. In addition, our owner may wish to approximate the decline in his firm's one-year-older plant and equipment by "charging himself" as depreciation a fraction (let us say 10 percent) of the equipment's original cost. Deducting these charges from gross revenues, that portion of the firm's overall cash flow from operations that is properly charged to each, and the remainder that flows through to net income, or earnings, can be summarized on the firm's income statement, as shown in Table 1-2.

Table 1-2 INCOME STATEMENT, "ALPHA CORPORATION"

1966

Sales	$100,000
Cost of goods sold	—87,500
Operating cash flow	12,500
Depreciation	— 1,500*
Interest	— 1,000
Net income before taxes	10,000
Taxes	— 5,000
Net income after taxes (earnings)	$ 5,000*

*Note that depreciation and earnings together provide $6,500 of internally generated funds for reinvestment in the business or withdrawal by the owner as desired.

Note that unlike a balance sheet, an income statement deals entirely with flows over an interval of time rather than stocks of assets or liabilities at an instant in time. Moreover, its emphasis is on flows that accrue to the firm from operations rather than from capital transactions (such as increases in debt or the sale of assets). In the simple case considered here, for example, $5,000 in earnings and $1,500 in depreciation are made available to the firm from operations during the year.

One also should notice that an income statement tells us nothing about how these (or other) funds actually are used. By adding $5,000 to net worth and $1,500 to accrued depreciation on the firm's next year-end balance sheet, one should not imagine that pots of money or bank accounts bearing such labels come into existence; for both are semifictitious "accrual," as distinct from "cash," charges that are levied by the firm against itself. Should one wish to look beneath such items for a fuller view of exactly *where* the firm's funds came from and *how* they were used during the year, a third type of financial report is helpful; this is called a *sources and uses statement* or a *funds flow statement*.

Sources and Uses Statement

Let us assume that during the year our entrepreneur increased his inventories by $2,000, drew down his cash balance by $500, spent nothing whatever on fixed assets, and met the initial $5,000 payment on his loan from the bank. His balance sheet by the end of December 1966, then, could be summarized as in column 2 of Table 1-3.

Table 1-3 **CONSOLIDATED BALANCE SHEET AND FUNDS FLOW STATEMENT, "ALPHA CORPORATION"**

December 31, 1965-6

	1965	1966	Successive Changes	Funds Source	Flows Use
ASSETS					
Current assets					
Cash	2,000	1,500	—500	500	
Inventories	8,000	10,000	+2,000		2,000
Total current	10,000	11,500	1,500		
Fixed assets					
Plant & equipment, gross	15,000	15,000	0	0	0
Accumulated depreciation	0	1,500	+1,500	**	**
Plant & equipment, net	15,000	13,500	—1,500	**	**
Land	10,000	10,000	0	0	0
Total fixed	25,000	23,500	—1,500	**	**
Total assets	35,000	35,000	0	0	0
LIABILITIES AND NET WORTH					
Current	5,000	5,000	0	0	0
Noncurrent	15,000	10,000	—5,000		5,000
Total liabilities	20,000	15,000	—5,000		
Net worth (from ownership)	15,000	20,000	+5,000	6,500*	
Total liabilities & net worth	35,000	35,000	0		
Total sources and uses of funds				7,000	7,000

* See income statement for the $6,500 total contribution from operations to the firm's cash flow (containing $5,000 classified for accounting purposes as earnings and $1,500 classified as depreciation).

** These changes between successive balance sheets are not carried forward to funds flow, as noncash or "accrual" items rather than actual cash flows are involved.

Although tables such as Tables 1-3 may be confusing at first sight, a fairly simple exercise, such as recording year-to-year changes in corresponding balance sheet items (as in column 3 of Table 1-3), can give a good initial indication of exactly *where* the firm's funds came from and *how* they were used over the period in question. We can translate changes in "cash items," such as inventories, debt, and cash itself, into those that *provide funds* (column 4 of Table 1-3) and those that *require funds* (column 5 of Table 1-3). Then to reconstruct quite accurately our entrepreneur's full array of funds—sources and uses—we can turn to the firm's income statement to find greater detail on funds generated from the firm's operations and underlying changes in various types of accrual items (such as depreciation, net plant and net worth categories).

Ratio Analyses

Each of the documents discussed (balance sheet, income, and funds flow statement) highlights a particular facet of the firm's financial situation and performance. None provides a comprehensive overview by itself, although when they are analyzed together one can obtain from them a reasonably complete and balanced view of the firm's structure and how it is changing over time. In combination with simple ratios—such as Current Assets/Current Liabilities to measure "liquidity"; Debt/Total Assets to measure longer term financial risk; and Net Income/Sales, or Net Income/Total Assets, to measure profitability—one can obtain from such documents a fairly optimistic appraisal of the Alpha Corporation's situation and progress.

During the first full year of its operation, the firm's liquidity, or current assets per dollar of current liabilities, clearly improved from $10,000/$5,000 = 2/1 to $11,500/$5,000 = 2.3/1.00. Similarly, by the careful husbanding of operating cash flows, its overall debt position was reduced from $20,000/$35,000 = 57 percent of total assets, to $15,000/$35,000 = 43 percent of total assets. Should existing profit rates, such as the firm's $12,500/$100,000 = 12.5 percent gross margin, and $5,000/$35,000 = 14 percent return on assets be maintained, further improvements in the company's safety, liquidity and value to its owners—or future balance sheet positions—can safely be anticipated.

In addition to *tracking trends*, however, operating ratios also can provide a basis for forecasts of future funds (or other resources) needs, and a basis for evaluating the firm's effectiveness in directing and controlling its operations. To the extent that such reports are used to evaluate the performance of various persons or departments in an organization, their motivational importance—and therefore their feedback on the performance being monitored—may be considerable.

CONCLUSION

The managerial function, to somewhat oversimplify, consists of utilizing and analyzing information so as to organize resources to serve a specified objective. In this chapter we have described some of these information sources; in the chapters that follow we shall describe a few of the analytical techniques available to management for utilizing information in decision making.

Managerial economics conventionally has stressed the concepts underlying these analytical techniques. To the best of its ability, managerial economics has focused on the development of tools for finding an optimal, or best, solution, given some specified objective. Defining that objective may not always be easy, but managerial economics presupposes that somehow or other the objective can be specified. Indeed, managerial economists feel most comfortable if the objective can be defined as profit maximization which, roughly translated, means making the most possible money for the owners of the firm, given the resources available. They recognize that this objective may not always be the most socially responsible. Sometimes compromises and other objectives must be entertained. But managerial economists would argue that their analytical techniques, even given these limitations, make a contribution to improving the productivity or efficiency of their enterprises. Furthermore, they would insist, with considerable propriety, that by trying to be efficient, their firm will contribute more to the wealth available to all groups in society than if it pursued other, more ambiguous goals.

This book, in essence, attempts to provide concisely an elementary introduction to the concepts of managerial economics and a relatively small number of related, operational tools. It does not cover all the topics that might be included under the heading of "managerial economics." It does not cover all topics in the depth that would be desirable or, indeed, even needed to expose certain important limitations on some of the techniques. It does, however, provide an introduction to an interesting and rapidly evolving field.

Marginal Analysis

CHAPTER TWO

BASIC CONCEPTS

The core of managerial economics historically has been the application of *marginal analysis* to determine optimal solutions for specific managerial problems. Marginal analysis, and its related theory of the firm, have roots deep in the mathematical calculus. The basic concepts, however, can be explained readily in nonmathematical terms.

The essential notion underlying all marginal analysis is that the search for an optimum or best possible position can be attained by trading, at the margin, one small additional quantity for another. Thus, assume that we want to maximize net revenues, what we called "net income after taxes (earnings)" on the income statement described in Chapter One. To do this for one given product, the business manager should continually compare the additional sales and revenues and costs he realizes or incurs by making small changes in the product's output level. As long as *small* increases in output add more to the firm's revenues than to its costs, *marginal revenues* can be said to be greater than *marginal costs* and *additional* units of output can be seen to be profitable.

Similarly, should labor or capital resources be transferred from the production of one good to another, marginal *additions* to revenue from the second good must be offset against marginal *losses* in revenue from the first. Should the additions be larger than the losses, the effect of the transfer is to increase the firm's profitability. Similarly, should small amounts of one resource (such as capital) be substituted for small amounts of another (such as labor) to produce the same level of output, the additional costs *incurred* by increasing one's use of the first resource must be offset against costs *saved* by reducing the use of the second. Again, should the cost savings be greater than the cost increases "at the margin," the transfer will be profitable and presumably desirable; if not, the transfer should not be undertaken.

In general, marginal comparisons such as these are not limited to specific, discrete choices at particular levels of output or specific resource combinations. Rather they are pursued continuously until all favorable transfers or tradeoffs have been adopted and optimal output levels or resource combinations have been obtained. For example, if a product's marginal revenue is greater than its marginal cost at a particular level of output and a production increase is profitable, then a *further* increase at the *new* margin may be desirable, and again at a still higher output level, until finally, marginal revenue no longer exceeds marginal cost and further increases in output no longer add to the firm's profitability.

One could, if he wished, visualize this decision process of trading at the margin as resembling that adopted by a myopic mountain climber (say Mr. Magoo) who doesn't know precisely where or how far away the top of the hill (the optimum) may be and does not care. He is confident, however, that as long as he goes uphill, he will eventually get to the summit. For the business manager, the hill's *height* is measured in units of profit rather than distance above sea level; its *gradient* is called *marginal profit* (which, in turn, is the difference between marginal revenue and marginal cost). As long as marginal revenue is greater than marginal cost, of course, their difference

$$\text{marginal profit} = \text{marginal revenue} - \text{marginal cost}$$

is positive, and the course of action of our myopic decision maker is well defined—output should be increased. When finally he reaches the summit there is, of course, no place else to go. His profit gradient is zero; marginal cost and marginal revenue are identically equal to each other (by definition), and an optimum output level has been obtained.

The basic concept is very simple and very general. However, in rough terrain containing more than one peak, or *local optimum*, it is potentially misleading. Then one faces the problem of deciding whether one is at the highest of attainable summits or just on top of a foothill. Fortunately, there are simple mathematical tests for making this determination. But they need not detain us here.

For our present purposes, it is necessary to note only that the marginal or incremental evaluations provide us with a decision rule for evaluating the possible tradeoffs available to a firm between different courses of action. As long as the marginal relationships between different tradeoffs are not equal to one another, it benefits a firm to make some changes. Thus, if one additional unit of output increases revenues more than it increases costs, it pays the firm to increase its level of output. Similarly, if the wage costs associated with an increase in labor inputs are less than the capital costs required to increase output by an identical amount, it pays the firm to use more labor and less capital to achieve any increase in production. Or if marginal revenues obtained per unit of cost from one product are greater than those obtained from another, it pays the firm to transfer resources from the production of one good to the other. At the margin, therefore, a firm's operations are *optimally balanced* only when such favorable tradeoffs no longer exist, that is, when these marginal tradeoffs are equalized all around.

The key terms, then, are *tradeoffs* and *equalization of margins*. And the purpose, stated once again, is to achieve an *optimum,* either in the form of maximum net profits or minimum costs. To develop these marginal concepts further, we shall next consider two illustrative applications commonly encountered in business: the pricing decision and inventory management.

BASIC PRICE AND OUTPUT DECISIONS

Price and output determination have conventionally been the central focus of the economist's theory of the firm. Price theory and the theory of the firm have been described elsewhere in this series.[1] Accordingly, only the more rudimentary aspects of this theory, and then only that which is most pertinent to business decision making, will be repeated here.

In the conventional theory of the firm, price is determined by juxtaposing demand and cost curves for the firm. The demand curves descibe how many units of a specified product can be sold by the firm at different prices. The cost curves describe the costs incurred by the firm at different output levels. In general, one expects unit or *average* costs to decline as output is increased from very low levels of output. Increases in output improve capacity utilization, permitting fixed costs, or *overhead,* to be spread over greater quantities of output; this, in turn, usually reduces average cost per unit of output. Eventually, though, capacity may be strained if output continues to expand; overtime may be necessary or less efficient resources may be employed. The result, presumably, will be the characteristically U-shaped average, and marginal cost to output relationships or *curves* illustrated in Fig. 2-1. As long as the marginal cost of producing an *additional* unit of output is less than the average cost of producing that level of output, increases in production will lead to lower average, or unit, production costs. Conversely, should marginal costs exceed average costs, increases in output will increase average, or unit, costs. Accordingly, average and marginal costs can be equal only when average cost is at its minimum, as illustrated in Fig. 2-1.

---

[1] Robert Dorfman, *The Price System* and *Prices and Markets,* two other volumes in this series.

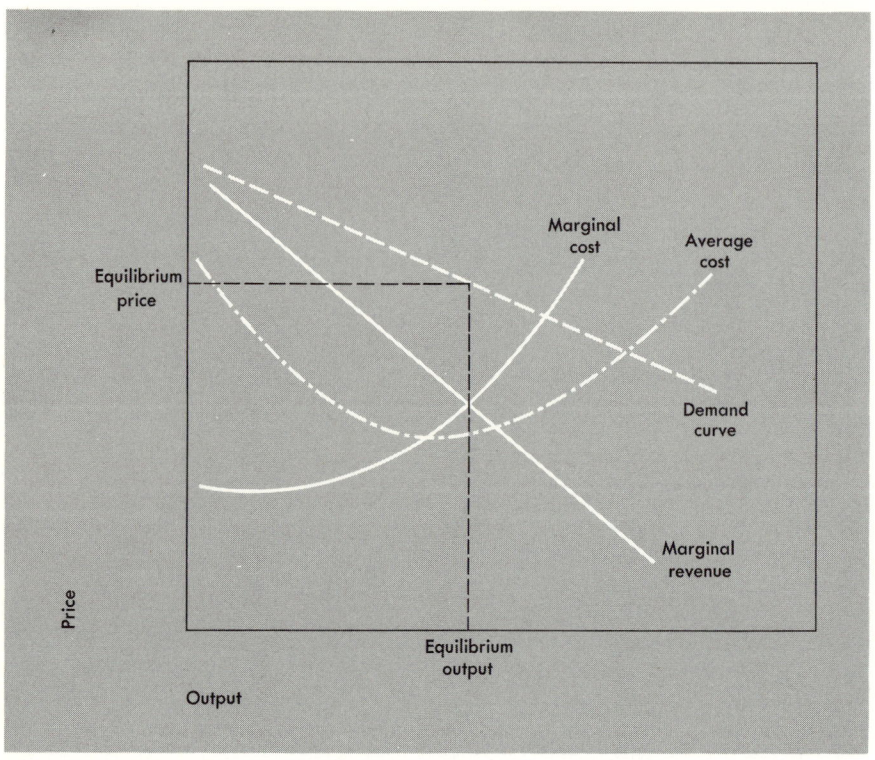

FIG. 2-1. Equilibrium price- and cost-output relationships for the firm.

If the firm is a small producer among many in a highly competitive market offering a standardized product, it is generally assumed, quite realistically, that the firm will have no control whatever over the price at which its goods can be sold. An individual wheat farmer is a classic example of a seller in such a market. Many businessmen, however, can increase the quantity of goods produced and sold only by reducing the price at which the goods are offered.

Diagramatically, this ability to affect sales volume by varying price would be expressed by a demand curve that slopes downward from left to right. The slope of the curve measures the extent to which a firm, by lowering its price, is able to increase the level of its sales or, conversely, the extent to which increases in price will restrict its level of output. A downward sloping demand curve with these properties is illustrated by the dashed line in Fig. 2-1.

The downward slope of the demand curve also means that price and marginal revenue cannot be identical to one another; for when prices are reduced to stimulate sales, new revenues from new customers are at least partially offset by reduced revenues from older customers, who would have continued to pay higher prices had they been so charged. Netting out the two effects produces the *marginal revenue* per unit of sales; this will be less, and perhaps much less, than the price of average revenue obtained for the same unit. Indeed, the marginal revenue curve must lie everywhere below the corresponding demand or average revenue curve, as illustrated in Fig. 2-1.

A major problem for management is to identify and obtain the proper cost and demand information for making a particular decision, considering the circumstances actually confronting the firm. In practice, this normally consists of accurately recognizing the all important differences between full and marginal costs, and between price and marginal revenues. Let us stress that the underlying principle of all marginal analysis as applied to pricing and output decisions is the same, and quite universally valid: output should be increased as long as additions to costs incurred are less than additions to revenues obtained; conversely, output and sales should be reduced if marginal costs exceed marginal revenue until the inequality is eliminated. The primary problem ordinarily encountered in practice is not one of concept—for the validity of the underlying marginal principle generally is not questioned—but is that of accurately identifying and measuring the *marginal costs* and *marginal revenues* for a particular product or business decision. In the next section some of these problems of identification and measurement are further illustrated.

MULTIPLE MARKETS, PRICE DISCRIMINATION AND GOVERNMENT REGULATION

Oftentimes business organizations, public and private, sell their wares or services in markets with decidedly different demand characteristics. In terms of the analytical structure just described, this would mean that more than one set of demand and cost curves would need to be defined for making the pricing decision.

One of the most common of such situations is that of a service for which demand varies sharply between time periods, say hours of the day or seasons of the year. Markets for electricity, transportation, home heating and cooking fuels are particularly obvious and pronounced illustrations of such *peaking* phenomena. The demand for electricity, for example, tends to vary widely at different hours of the day, usually peaking at some time around five to six P.M. and reaching a low point in the early morning hours. Markets for electricity therefore will be used here to illustrate the analytical problems of these markets in general, though it should be recognized that the principles apply far more widely.

A pricing problem arises in situations of fluctuating demands because the costs associated with serving the different markets, peak and off-peak, often differ substantially. For example, the provision of electricity usually requires large investments in what is called *fixed plant*. Indeed, the capital costs associated with providing this fixed plant are generally a substantial share of the total unit costs. For analytical purposes, it is generally assumed that the cost of providing a unit of electric service can be subdivided into two basic categories: operating costs (which we shall denote by OC) and capital costs (which we shall denote by CC). Furthermore, the usual convention is to assume that these two costs are more or less invariant, or constant, regardless of the volume of output. Thus, if TC represents total costs per unit of output then this total cost can be subdivided into operating costs per unit of output (OC) and capital costs per unit of output (CC), i.e., $TC = OC + CC$.

An extra, and economically fascinating, dimension is added to the electric utility problem by the fact that electric utilities are normally under some form of government regulation or, in some cases, of actual public ownership. This arises from the fact that electric utilities are generally considered to be a *natural monopoly*. (In essence, natural monopoly is the term used to characterize an industry where only one firm can be in the market efficiently at one point in time.)

Regulators, or managers of publicly owned electric utilities, usually accept as their goal the sale of as much of the service as possible while still covering the basic cost of providing that service. (In order to greatly simplify the semantics and complexities of the analysis, let it be assumed that these costs include some form of fair return on the capital invested in the utility.) Determining the prices that will maximize the use of a service while still covering all costs is a classic problem in marginal analysis. It is also a problem that illustrates the need to define carefully the relevant margins involved in marginal analyses.

To illustrate the analytical problems involved, let us assume that a market exists for which two demand functions can be defined, one of which pertains to peak utilization periods and one to all other periods. As before, let the costs of servicing these markets be decomposable into operating costs and capital costs, OC and CC, which are invariant to output. The relevant cost and demand information might be summarized as in Fig. 2-2 wherein all the labels have been defined before except D_o, which represents the off-peak demand function, and D_p which represents the peak period demand function. It should be noted that in this regulated price environment, no marginal revenue curves are needed because the demand or average revenue curve is also the marginal revenue curve. In this particular, and highly simplified, case the pricing and output solutions which will achieve maximum output while meeting all costs are quite easy to determine. Specifically, users during the peak period should be charged a price equal to total cost per unit, that is, the sum of the constant operating costs and capital cost, and the peak period output, shown in Fig. 2-2, is X_p. For the off-peak period the price should be set at a level to just cover the operating costs, and output would be at the level X_o.

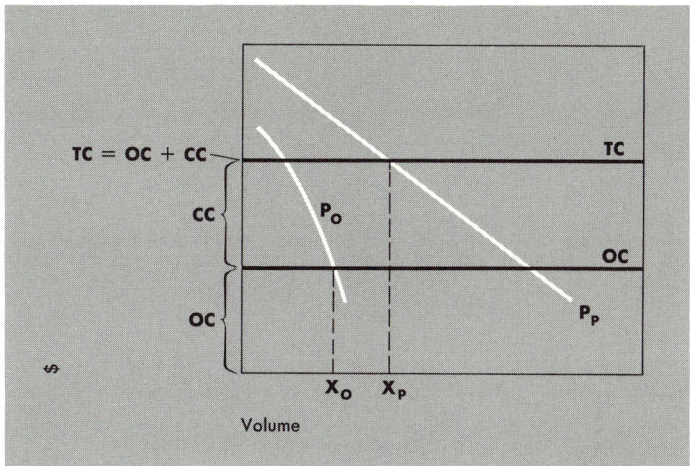

FIG. 2-2

However, complications can sometimes arise. In Fig. 2-2 the demand for off-peak periods lies everywhere below that for peak periods. In some cases, if one were to charge only operating costs to off-peak users, they could demand more than the peak period users who are charged the higher price equal to the sum of operating costs and capital costs. This perverse situation is illustrated in Fig. 2-3 wherein X_o is to the right and therefore larger than X_p, just reversing the situation in Fig. 2-2. In short, by charging

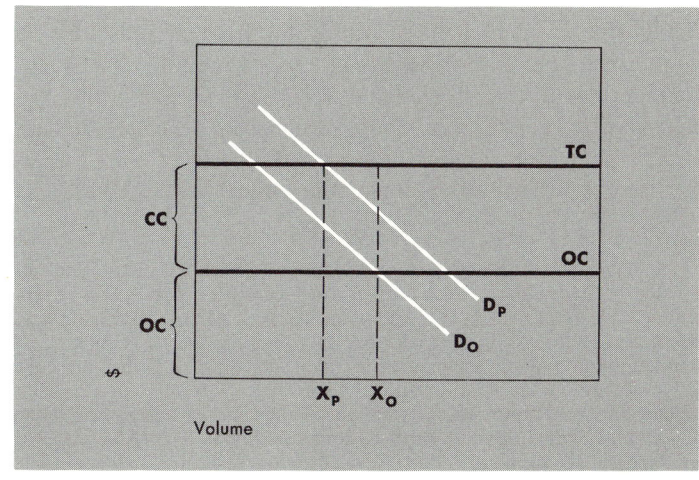

FIG. 2-3

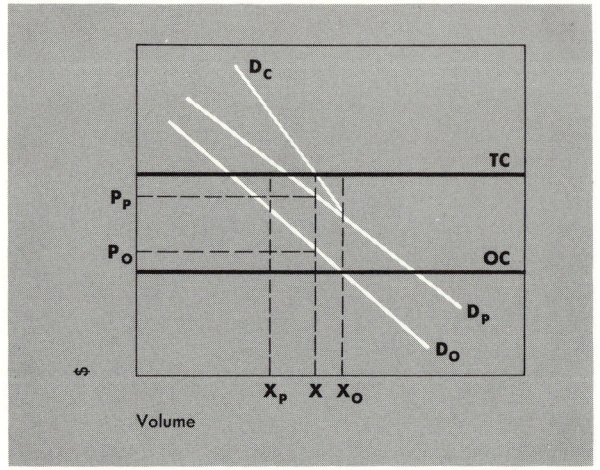

FIG. 2-4

all the capacity costs to the peak users only and charging only operating costs to the off-peak users one has created a situation in which the demand during the off-peak actually dominates or exceeds that of the peak period.

The analytical solution to this problem is actually quite simple (though it took ecoomists some time to discover it).[2] The trick is to add the different demand curves vertically. Specifically, one should add the off-peak demand curve D_o to the peak curve D_p for all portions of the demand curve D_o above the price equal to operating costs. (Portions of the demand curve below this price level are irrelevant since under no circumstances according to the rules would one be willing to charge someone less than the operating costs of the service he uses.) The intersection of this combined or total demand curve with the total cost curve, TC, determines the level of output which one is justified in providing for both periods; this would be the level of output denoted by X in Fig. 2-4, where D_c is the combined, or total, demand curve, that is, the sum of D_o and D_t above the minimum price level determined by OC. The prices which can be charged to peak and off-peak users and which will cover exactly all costs of this level of output are determined by the intersection of the output level X with each demand curve;

---

[2] Probably the earliest exposition in English of the solution to this problem was by Peter O. Steiner, "Peak Loads and Efficient Pricing," *The Quarterly Journal of Economics* (November 1957), pp. 585-610. Earlier presentations of the solution can, however, be found in French. See particularly Marcel Boiteux, "La tarification des demandes en pointe; application de la théorie de la vente au coût marginal," *Revue Générale de l'Electricité* (August 1949), pp. 321-340. An English translation of this article and other important contributions by French engineering-economists to pricing and capital budgeting theory can be found in James R. Nelson, ed., *Marginal Cost Pricing in Practice* (Englewood Cliffs, N.J.: Prentice-Hall, Inc., 1964).

thus P_p would be the price for the peak period and P_o would be the price for the off-peak period. These prices are such that they would cover the cost, both operating and capacity, and would fully utilize the total available capacity during both periods.

Of course, if one wished to play by a different set of rules, say those of strict profit maximization, instead of by "regulated" pricing policies, one would also need the marginal revenue curves for each demand curve. Output, as stated earlier, should be set so that at the margin, revenues equal costs (on the last unit of output); this profit maximizing output would, though, be less than the "regulated" output since the marginal revenue curves would be everywhere below the demand curves. Again, though, a shifting peak is possible with the marginal revenue curves, just as with the demand curves diagrammed in Figs. 2-3 and 2-4. In this case, one would have to add vertically the marginal revenue curves instead of the demand curves in order to determine the level of output which would maximize profits; the peak and off-peak prices which would correspond to this profit maximizing output could be read from the relevant demand curves.

It is not the purpose here, though, to explain all the complications and possibilities that one might encounter when multiple markets and price discrimination are involved. The point, rather, is to illustrate the general flexibility of using demand and cost curves as aids to managerial pricing decisions and the importance of correctly defining these curves in actual applications.

THE INVENTORY LOT SIZE PROBLEM

One of the simplest and most useful applications of marginal analysis to business decisions relates to inventory policy, specifically to the so-called inventory lot-size problem. In this case marginal optimization leads to the relatively well known square root rule. This rule states that the optimal lot size for a firm's orders of additions to inventory will be proportional not to sales themselves but to the square root of the firm's sales over a specified period of time.[3]

The model can be summarized briefly as follows. Assume that: (1) sales and delivery lead times are known with certainty; (2) inventory carrying costs (which will be defined more precisely below) are directly proportional to inventories on hand; and (3) the purchase cost of a given quantity of goods to be held in inventory contains both a *fixed cost* element that *does not* vary with the purchase's size, and a *variable cost* element that *does* vary (proportionally) with its size. With these definitions and as-

---

[3] T. M. Whitine, *The Theory of Inventory Management,* 2nd ed. (Princeton, N.J.: Princeton University Press, 1957).

sumptions, all that is necessary to complete the analysis is a careful delineation of the various costs involved.

Specifically, let us express the total cost of procuring and holding a particular quantity of inventory in terms of two basic cost categories: first, the cost of actually purchasing the goods to be held (or the transaction costs, as they are usually called), and second, the cost of holding or carrying these goods, once obtained, until drawn into the production process. Some formal, mathematical notation can be helpful at this point; so let us define:

q as the *quantity,* or number of units ordered in each inventory lot, i.e., the lot size;

S as the *sales,* or number of units of the inventoried item consumed during a particular period of time (a year, for example);

n as the *number* of separate orders placed during each period of time (note that $n = S/q$ follows by definition);

f as the constant, or *fixed,* cost incurred each time an order is placed, no matter how large or small the order may be (so that such a cost, presumably, would derive from the administrative, clerical, and posting expenses unavoidably associated with an order's processing);

v as the price, or *variable,* cost of purchasing each unit q of the commodity ordered;

h as the *holding* cost per unit q of inventory stocked during the period of time; and

C_t, C_o, C_h as, respectively, the *total* annual cost, *ordering* cost, and *holding* cost, resulting from a particular inventory lot size or ordering policy.

Relying on this notation, we can now express the cost of placing a single order for q units of a commodity quite simply as the sum of its fixed and variable cost elements, $f + vq$. Thus, suppose that 100 units of a widget costing 10¢ each are desired for inventory purposes, and that it costs the firm $2.00 in administrative expenses simply to process such an order. Then the overall costs resulting from a single order or transaction for 100 widgets could be written as

$$f + vq = \$2.00 + \$0.10(100) = \$12.00.$$

Should 100 units constitute only 10 percent of the firm's annual sales, then S would equal 1000 which would be the total annual unit requirement for these widgets. Thus, 10 orders of 100 would be required each year, and the firm's *annual ordering costs* under a $q = 100$ unit lot size policy would be calculated as

$$C_o = \frac{S}{q}[f + vq] = n[f + vq]$$
$$= 10[\$2.00 + \$0.10(100)] = \$120.00$$

(Eq. 2-1)

By increasing the number of units q obtained in each lot, of course, the firm can reduce the number of transactions required—and therefore the number of $2.00 fixed costs incurred—during any particular period of time.

By placing only one such order each year for its entire $q = 1,000$ unit annual needs, for example, the firm could reduce the annual cost of orders from $120 to $102. Going even further and placing a single order for several years of widget needs, the firm presumably could reduce its annual ordering costs to as close an approximation as desired to the $100 theoretical minimum dictated by variable costs alone. The entire schedule of alternative *lot size* and *annual ordering cost* combinations can be plotted as the solid, downward sloping curve in Fig. 2-5.

Even in the absence of uncertainty about future inventory needs, however, no firm would be likely to go so far as to stockpile several years supply of widgets, and for good reasons. It costs money to provide the capital, warehouse space, policing, supervision, auditing, insurance, etc., required to hold such an inventory, and presumably it should cost more to carry large rather than small inventories. Let's assume, for simplicity, that inventory *holding costs* rise proportionally with the number of units held, say by h dollars per unit/per year. Let us further assume that widgets are drawn from inventory into production at a fairly uniform rate, and that as a result approximately half of each *order quantity*, or $q/2 = 50$ units, are held on

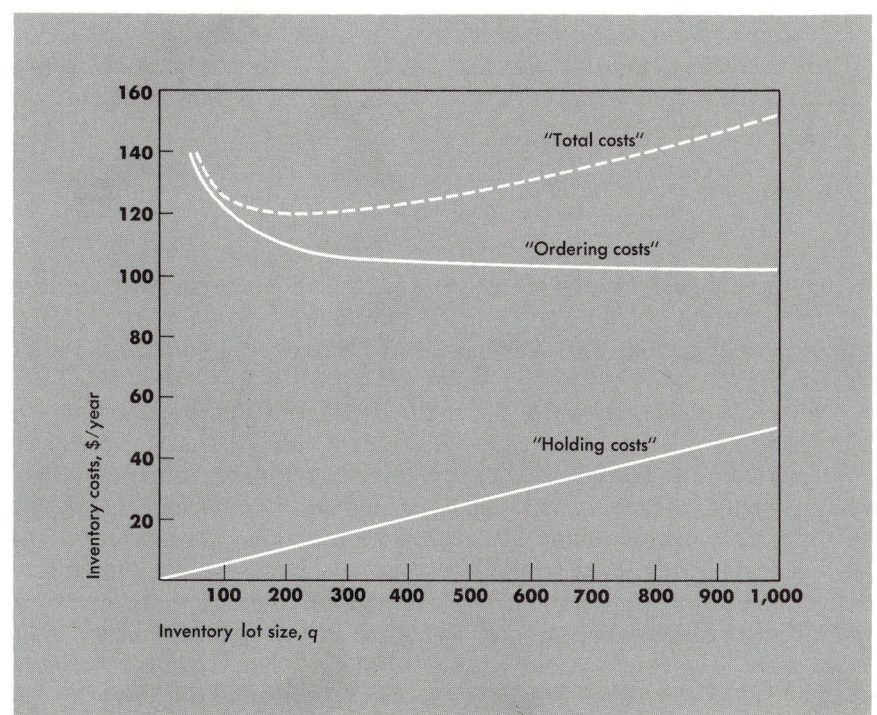

FIG. 2-5 Graphical solution, inventory lot size problem.

the average in the company's inventory stock over the course of a year. Relying again on our previous notation, annual inventory holding costs can then be expressed simply as the product of *unit holding costs* times the *average number of units held*, or as

$$C_h = h\frac{q}{2}. \qquad \text{(Eq. 2-2)}$$

Should unit holding costs for our hypothetical firm's widget amount to $h = \$.10$ (or 10¢ per widget per year), aggregate holding costs under a $q = 100$ unit order policy would amount to approximately

$$C_h = \$.10 \left(\frac{100}{2}\right) = \$5.00 \text{ per year.}$$

Similarly, annual holdings costs under a $q = 200$ unit order quantity could be calculated as $C_h = \$.10 \frac{200}{2} = \$10.00$ per year; and under a $q = 400$ unit policy as $C_h = \$.10 \frac{400}{2} = \$20.00$ per year. The whole schedule of possible lot size-holding cost combinations can be quickly sketched as the upward sloping straight line labelled "holding costs" in Fig. 2-5.

By combining Eq. 2-1 and Eq. 2-2 the total costs associated with a particular inventory order policy, or lot size q, can be expressed as the sum of annual ordering and holding costs, or as

$$C_t = C_o + C_h = \frac{S}{q}[f + vq] + h\frac{q}{2}. \qquad \text{(Eq. 2-3)}$$

For our illustrative example, these costs amount to $125 per year under a 100 unit ordering policy. The complete schedule of possible lot size and total cost combinations are diagrammed as the dashed U-shaped curve in Fig. 2-5.

Just as it is clear from Eq. 2-1 that a decision to increase inventory lot sizes will *reduce* the frequency with which orders must be placed, and therefore the fixed costs associated with inventory transactions (ordering costs) over any period of time, so also should it now be clear (from Eq. 2-2 and Fig. 2-5) that such an action will *increase* the average quantity of inventories held and therefore the carrying costs associated with storage, insurance, etc., or simply with inventory holdings. Herein, of course, lies the nub of a classical resource allocation problem. The task of our decision maker, most simply stated, is to determine the level q, or lot size which *optimally balances* these conflicting forces, so as to minimize the total costs associated with his inventory policy over any period of time.

A mathematician, invoking the differential calculus, could solve Eq. 2-3 directly for the lot size q whose value minimizes total inventory costs, once sales (S), fixed ordering costs (f), and unit holding costs (h) are known. The resulting solution involves a quadratic expression in q that, on simplification, reduces to the square root rule, relating optimal inventory order quantities (q) to the square root of the firms sales (S), that is,

$$q = \sqrt{2\frac{f}{h}S}. \qquad \text{(Eq. 2-4)}$$

On application to our illustrative problem, the formula suggests that a $q = 100$ unit ordering policy is rather low; for the firm's optimal lot size, given its cost structure, turns out to be approximately

$$q = \sqrt{2\frac{2}{.1} \cdot 1{,}000} = 200 \text{ units.}$$

Less mathematically oriented persons, however, might approach the problem's solution graphically as in Fig. 2-5. First, they could construct the required ordering cost curve; it would decline as lot size q increases. Similarly, carrying or holding cost could be shown as a straight line that increases with lot size. These two curves could then be combined or added to produce a total cost curve whose minimum would be the hypothetical problem's 20 unit optimal order quantity.

However the solution is attempted, whether analytically as in Eq. 2-4, or graphically as in Fig. 2-5, the basic principles that emerge are quite familiar. Again, the decision turns on the balancing of margins. In this case, the trick is to increase lot size until marginal reductions in transactions costs are exactly balanced by marginal increases in carrying costs. At this point, of course, total annual inventory costs will be minimized effectively.

It remains to convert lot size into a time profile of inventory stockholdings. Say these displayed the smooth, saw-toothed pattern illustrated in Fig. 2-6; this implies that as inventories are worked down to reorder points at a uniform rate, they are replenished by orders of lot size q. To determine a sensible reorder point, however, it will be useful to consider the possibility that businessmen may wish to hold safety stocks—to protect themselves, say, against the possibility of lost sales resulting from unexpectedly being out of stock. Should one be able to forecast without error *both* the rate at which widgets will be consumed from inventory *and* the delivery lead time required for their replenishment, safety margins such as that represented by reorder point m in Fig. 2-6 would not be necessary. In the absence of an ability to foresee perfectly either the exact timing of sales or the elapsed time between order and delivery, however, some positive safety margin may be in order. The size of this safety margin would be determined in several (increasingly complex) ways: (1) completely intuitively; (2) on the intuitive selection of an out-of-stock probability, such as the decision maker's willingness to accept one chance in fifty of being caught out-of-stock; or (3) on

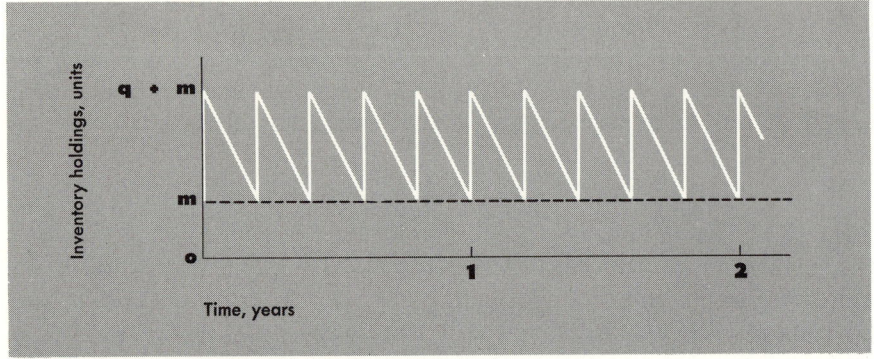

FIG. 2-6 Inventory holdings, time profile.

expected cost minimization, using analytical techniques such as those considered in Chapter Five.

For retail establishments, lot size and safety stock considerations may exhaust the inventory problem. For manufacturing firms, on the other hand, both may be minor in comparison to the importance of uncoupling production from seasonal or other foreseeable sales fluctuations. Tradeoffs between the costs incurred by seasonably varying production, and the risks and costs inherent in production smoothing are, to say the least, nontrivial. Like most such problems, this issue is more easily raised and illustrated than solved.

CONCLUSION

The uses of marginal analysis in business problem solving are hardly exhausted by the illustrative pricing and inventory problems discussed in the present chapter. Indeed, the basic concepts of marginal analysis underlie almost all optimization procedures used by managerial economists or operation researchers today. In the next two chapters increasingly complex applications of such analysis to business decisions will be described.

Mathematical Programming

CHAPTER THREE

MATHEMATICAL PROGRAMMING AND THE OPERATIONS RESEARCH APPROACH

Most rapidly developing fields are thought to contain at least two types of persons, those who are "with it" and those who are not. Managerial economics is no exception to this very general rule.

Those who are considered to be "with it" in managerial economics, or operations research as it is often called today, can be identified in part by their age (youth is thought to be a necessary, if not a sufficient, condition for vitality) and in part by their facility with computers and predilection for applied, operational problems. Other characteristics that set the new breed of operations research specialists apart from more conventional managerial economists include an almost evangelistic elan, a belief in the quantifiability of social, economic and technological relationships, relatively strong mathematical backgrounds, and a contempt for the paraphernalia that surrounds, if not for the concepts that underlie, classical economic theory. Terms such as "marginal revenue productivity," "opportunity cost," and "returns to scale" seldom occur in the professional jargon of operations researchers, although other terms that embody identical concepts are essential elements of their growing professional vocabularly.

Economists have played a prominent role in developing many of the operational techniques that are so familiar to operations research as we know it today—and with good reason. For whatever its application, operations research finds its *raison d'etre* in the optimal allocation of scarce resources. Whether one's objective is to *maximize* a strategic nuclear capability, the profitability of a manufacturer's product mix, or to *minimize* the number of highway fatalities per year, the cost of transporting goods from factories to warehouses, or of blending a wide variety of materials to create animal feeds or gasolines or sausages, the problems remain the same. Scarce resources committed to one use necessarily are withdrawn from another, and benefits obtained from one output may be enjoyed only at the cost of benefits foregone from others. Management's function, again, is to choose from among the (perhaps infinite) set of attainable input-output combinations, or marginal tradeoffs, that which is, in some sense, most desirable. Accordingly, an operations research specialist's function is to employ his analytic skills to assist responsible decision makers in the often difficult tasks of:

1. Accurately defining and quantifying the set of outputs attainable from an organization's (necessarily limited) pool of productive resources;
2. Quantifying to the extent possible, the organization's, or decision maker's, criteria for choice among these outputs; and
3. Deriving from 1. and 2. the operational implications of the firm's objectives and output possibilities by solving for an optimal solution to its resource allocation problem.

Operations research, then, shares the classical economist's emphasis on optimization but adds to this an emphasis on the *quantification* of underlying structural relationships, resource limitations, managerial objectives (or choice criteria), and *solves for* their operational implications in very precise and practical terms—so many units of X and so many units of Y should be used to *maximize* the profitability (or *minimize* the cost) of producing units of good A and β units of good B in such-and-such a fashion. In addition, a creative analyst will attempt to measure the sensitivity of his problem's solution to the many assumptions that have gone into its specification. How important is it to an organization, for example, to employ *exactly* X and Y units of resources to produce goods A and B in *exactly* the specified numbers? How much would be lost by producing a little less of A and correspondingly more of B? Or how much more could be obtained by relaxing one or more of the (physical, institutional, or financial) restrictions built into a particular problem's solution? Information of this sort, concerning changes in the ground rules under which resource allocation decisions take place, often are of greater use to creative managements than specific solutions for a specific, short range production, inventory or transportation problem. Mathematical programming is one of the basic tools that the operations researcher or modern managerial economist uses in meeting these responsibilities, as the greatly simplified but nevertheless typical problem in operations management presented in the next section serves to illustrate.

LINEAR PROGRAMMING: AN ILLUSTRATIVE EXAMPLE

Consider a company (or a division of a company, or a section of a division, etc.) whose sole purpose is to manufacture two types of products; call them Widget A and Widget B, or *A*utos and *B*uses, or whatever you like. (We shall henceforth use Widget A and auto and Widget B and bus interchangeably.) Suppose the company's cost accountants have determined the profit margin on Widget A (on autos) to be $300 per unit, and on B (on buses) to be $360 per unit. Suppose further that the company can sell as many extra units of each product as it can produce, hire as much extra labor, buy as many extra parts, and obtain as much extra capital as it needs, without affecting prices in any of the markets in which it buys or sells. The company's operating profit margins, then, may safely be presumed to be *constant* over the range of outputs contemplated.[1]

Should this be the end of the story, there would be neither a production nor a pricing problem. Our competitive model and a rational management would concur on the desirability, indeed on the optimality, of producing an *infinite* number of *both* types of goods. In practice, of course, most firms are likely to face some resource limitations long before adverse market movements are encountered. Their short run resource allocation problem, then, may be reduced simply to utilizing these limited resources as efficiently as possible.

Let us assume for illustrative purposes that our hypothetical firm's near term production possibilities are limited by only two effective restrictions. The firm possesses 1,000 units, however defined, of one type of facility—let us call it stamping capacity—and 2,000 units of assembly capacity. Let us further assume that Widget A requires 2 units of stamping capacity (machine hours, perhaps) and 5 units of assembly capacity, while Widget B requires 3 and 4 units, respectively, of stamping and assembly capacities. By adding the completely formal assumption that the firm is capable only of transforming inputs into outputs—and not the other way around—our problem is fully specified.

Should an operations analyst enter the picture at this point and verify that management's objective is to maximize the profits obtainable from its operations, he would have no difficulty at all expressing the problem, both succinctly and fully, in mathematical terms. Defining π as the firm's total operating profit, α as the (yet unknown) number of units of Widget A to be produced, β as the number of units of B, and recalling that $\leq$ and $\geq$ are

---

[1] Although such an assumption may seem (and be) unrealistic over a wide range of outputs, it may be perfectly serviceable for planning purposes by small firms, or by divisions of larger firms whose incremental effects on a total market are relatively small.

mathematical shorthand for "less than or equal to" and "greater than or equal to" statements, respectively, an analyst could summarize most of the preceding section in three, very basic sets of equations:

maximize

$$\pi = 300\alpha + 360\beta \qquad \text{(Eq. 3-1)}$$

subject to the following limitations,

$$2\alpha + 3\beta \leq 1{,}000 \quad \text{(stamping capacity is not exceeded)} \quad \text{(Eq. 3-2)}$$

$$5\alpha + 4\beta \leq 2{,}000 \quad \text{(assembly capacity is not exceeded)} \quad \text{(Eq. 3-3)}$$

and

$$\begin{matrix}\alpha \geq 0 \\ \beta \geq 0\end{matrix} \quad \text{only positive (or zero) outputs are feasible.} \quad \begin{matrix}\text{(Eq. 3-4)} \\ \text{(Eq. 3-5)}\end{matrix}$$

This is the standard format for a broad class of mathematical programming problems. Look it over carefully. It contains three types of statements. The first, Eq. 3-1, generally is called an *objective function*, for it summarizes the objective, or the choice criteria, or the net revenue, profit, benefit, utility, or whatever you wish to call it, whose value is to be *optimized*. In some cases, such as that considered here, *optimization* is synonymous with maximization; in other cases (e.g., where costs rather than benefits appear in Eq. 3-1) *optimization* may imply *minimization*. In any case, however, optimization requires a decision maker to select from the (perhaps infinite) set of attainable input-output combinations that one which is "best" in terms of his problem's objective (as specified in Eq. 3-1).

The word *attainable*, perhaps, requires emphasis. Our problem, as formulated, is not designed to optimize unconditionally. Dr. Pangloss' "Best of all possible worlds" it not sought. Rather, mathematical programming seeks to solve for the best of all *attainable* worlds.

Equations 3-2 through 3-5, in fact, distinguish attainable from unattainable production possibilities. Specifically, Eqs. 3-2 and 3-3 summarize a series of structural and capacity limitations that restrict management's freedom of choice among alternative production possibilities. Equation 3-2, for example, combines each product's technical need for stamping facilities with the firm's known, and finite, stamping capacity. More explicitly, Eq. 3-2 combines the respective needs of Widgets A and B for 2 and 3 units of stamping facilities per unit of output with the firm's 1,000 unit limit on available stamping facilities. Similarly, Eq. 3-3 formalizes the restriction on the production possibilities of our hypothetical firm because of its 2,000 unit limitation on assembly capacity.

In addition, Eqs. 3-4 and 3-5, the programming problem's so-called *non-negativity* restrictions, impose on our problem the very obvious fact (to an analyst, if not to a computer) that the path from inputs to outputs is one-way, i.e., although stamping and assembly facilities may be transformed into final products such as autos and buses, the reverse is not possible. One cannot purchase automobiles and buses (at $300 and $360 per unit, for example) and melt them down or otherwise transform them into additional units of stamping and assembly capacity.

Any problem that contains non-negativity restrictions (such as Eqs. 3-4 and 3-5) and permits direct solution for a precise optimum is called a *mathematical programming problem*. Moreover, should such a problem be characterized by both a *linear* objective function (such as Eq. 3-1) and a set of *linear* structural or capacity restrictions (such as Eqs. 3-2 and 3-3 above), it is said to be a *linear programming problem*.

Algebraically, an equation such as Eq. 3-1 is said to be linear in quantities a and β if the quantity that depends on them (here profit) varies only as a multiple of changes in either a or β. For example, profit is *linearly* related to automobile production if an increase in automobile output increases profit by a fixed number of dollars per unit, as by $300 *per unit of output* in the present example. Similarly, profit is *linearly* related to bus production in Eq. 3-1 if an increase in output increases profit by a fixed number of dollars, such as $360 *for each additional bus produced*. And finally, if a function, such as Eq. 3-1, is linear in *all* its arguments (e.g., automobiles, buses, cabbages, and pears, etc.), it is said simply to be a *linear equation*. Note that Eqs. 3-2 and 3-3 also are linear relationships, specifically, linear *inequalities* by such a definition.

Graphically, a linear relationship possesses the extremely convenient property that it is described by a straight line (hence the word "linear") in any (and all) its dimensions. For example, the straight line labelled $100,000 in Fig. 3-1 connects all possible combinations of Widgets A and B whose production (at margins of $300 and $360 per unit, respectively) yields *exactly* $100,000 in operating profit for our hypothetical firm per month, year, or other (postulated) period of time. The line, which we may call an *equal profit curve*, is in fact a special case (where profit is held constant at $\pi =$ 100,000) of a broad class of possible, graphical representations for Eq. 3-1. The line, or function, illustrates, for example, that with a profit margin of $300 per unit, 333 units of Widget A are required to yield $100,000 *if only A is produced* (the point of intersection on the horizontal axis). Similarly, 278 units of Widget B are required (at an operating profit margin of $360) to yield $100,000 in operating profit *if no units of A and only units of B are produced*. In addition, however, the curve also tells us that half as many units of A and B together (specifically, 167 units of A *and* 139 units of B) also can produce $100,000 in operating profit, as can any other *"linearly related* combination of automobiles and buses *on the $100,000 curve."*

As one moves from one point to another on the curve, it quickly becomes apparent that $360/300 = 1.2$ additional units of A always are re-

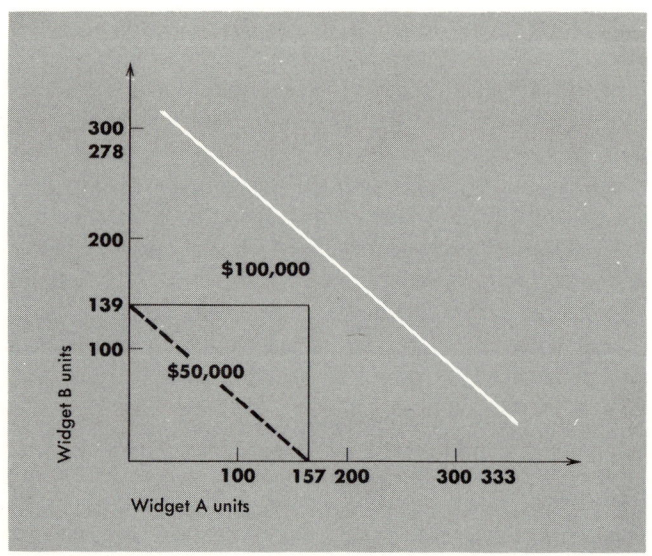

FIG. 3-1 Equal profit output combinations.

quired to make up for the profit lost by a unit reduction in the company's output of Widget B. Turning the same statement around, the profit obtainable from 1 additional unit of A is worth that attainable from 300/360 = .83 units of B, and the company's equal profit curve, accordingly, will be a straight line whose slope, summarizing B's value in terms of A, equals −.83 throughout.

A similar curve connecting 167 units of Widget A on the horizontal axis and 139 units of B on the vertical axis could be drawn to represent the whole family of output combinations yielding $50,000 in operating profit per month, week, or year, as the case may be. This curve, too, exhibits the constant 300/360 = .83 marginal tradeoff between profit per unit of A and B and, accordingly, is parallel to (but half the distance from the origin as) the firm's $100,000 equal profit curve. Similar curves, clearly, can be drawn for any other "equal profit level" on Fig. 3-1's "output axes."

Our hypothetical firm, like any real life firm, however, is not interested in every possible equal profit curve but in only one—the highest attainable! Before this can be found, however, it will be necessary to diagram the limitations summarized in Eqs. 3-2 through 3-5, i.e., the firm's *attainable* production possibilities must be defined.

Recall that our firm possesses exactly 1,000 units of stamping capacity, neither more nor less. From the information discussed earlier and summarized in Eq. 3-2, then, we know that

$$1{,}000 = 2\alpha + 3\beta$$

(Eq. 3-2a)

MATHEMATICAL PROGRAMMING

defines the set of *maximum* output combinations whose stamping requirements do not exceed the total amount of capacity available. We also notice that, like an equal profit curve, Eq. 3-2 is a linear equation and, accordingly, defines a negatively sloped straight line on a diagram such as Fig. 3-1. The firm, clearly, can produce no more than $\alpha = 1000/2$ units of Widget A if only A is produced, or $\beta = 1000/3$ units of Widget B if only B is produced —or any linear combination of the two if part of its stamping capacity is devoted to each.

Similarly, with 2,000 units of assembly capacity, we see from Eq. 3-3 that,

$$2{,}000 = 5\alpha + 4\beta \qquad \text{(Eq. 3-3a)}$$

defines the set of maximum output combinations attainable within the firm's assembly capacity limitation. This "frontier" also can be defined by a negatively sloped straight line from $\alpha = 2000/5 = 400$ if only A's or autos are produced, to $\beta = 2000/4 = 500$ if assembly capacity is devoted entirely to B's, or bus production.

It is clear, then, that Widget A's *cost* in terms of stamping facilities is (from either Eq. 3-2 or Eq. 3-2a) two-thirds of Widget B's, and in terms of assembly facilities is (from Eq. 3-3 or Eq. 3-3a) five-fourths Widget B's. We can, of course, set either stamping capacity or assembly capacity to any level we like and produce a family of *equal capacity* curves which, like the family of equal profit curves, can be characterized by a constant slope reflecting relative resource costs, while distance from the origin reflects total levels of the resource consumed.

Once again, management is not likely to care a great deal about the allocative implications of a broad range of alternative resource levels but will be vitally interested in the limits imposed by current (or contemplated) resource capacities on the firm's production possibilities. In Fig. 3-2, therefore, the graphical implications of our hypothetical firm's 1,000 units of stamping capacity and 2,000 units of assembly capacity are separately depicted. Were assembly to constitute the firm's only effective resource limitation, it would be apparent from Fig. 3-2 that as many as 500 ($=2000/4$) units of Widget B or 400 ($=2000/5$) units of Widget A would be attainable, were *none* of the other product to be produced. So also would half the firm's maximum production of both commodities (in this case, 250 units of B *and* 200 units of A) be attainable, as would any other combination of outputs lying *on or below* the assembly capacity curve. Similar statements, clearly, are possible for the firm's 1,000 unit stamping capacity limitation. The fact that our firm can exceed *neither* capacity restriction, however, guarantees that its actual production possibilities are limited to the area on or below the *heavy* curve outlining the *lesser of* assembly or stamping capacity limitations for any output combination.

At this point the non-negativity restrictions also must be brought into

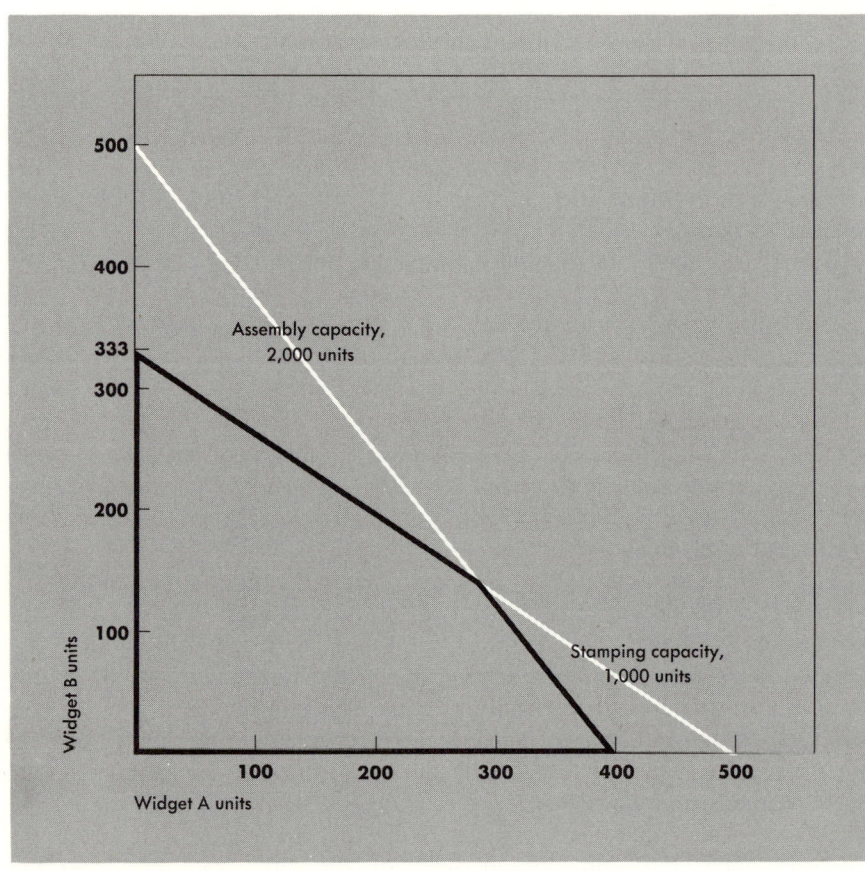

FIG. 3-2 Obtainable output combinations, or production possibilities.

play. Their effect, geometrically, is to further limit the firm's production possibilities to the region *above* the horizontal axis ($\beta \geq 0$) and to the *right of* the veritcal axis $a \geq 0$). As we shall see in a moment, when Fig. 3-1's criterion for choosing between alternative output combinations is combined with Fig. 3-2's definition of attainable production possibilities to select the *best attainable* output combination, this set of seemingly trivial restrictions plays an important mathematical, as well as economic, role.

Before combining Figs. 3-1 and 3-2 to solve our hypothetical resource allocation problem, let us pursue for a moment some of the economic implications of the graphical constructs we have depicted. First, it is apparent from Fig. 3-1 that the slope of a given equal profit curve defines the rate at which one product can be traded off against another in terms of profitability. It also is apparent from Fig. 3-2 that the slope of a given equal capacity curve defines the rate at which products may be traded off against

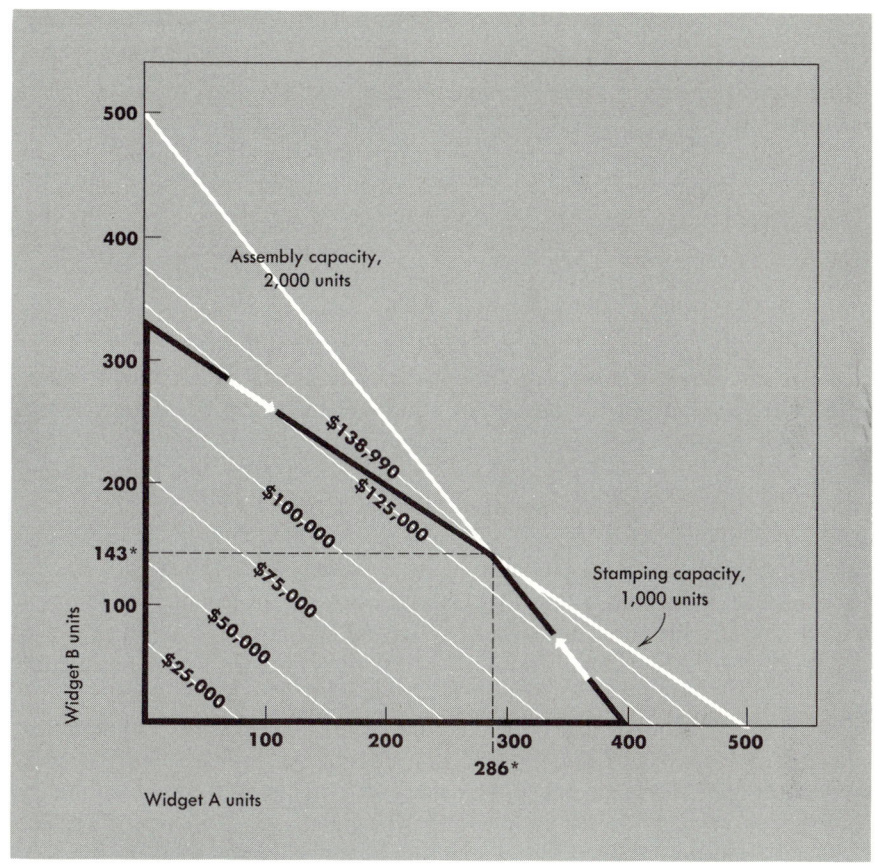

FIG. 3-3 Graphical solution, optimal product mix.

one another in terms of capacity utilization. Combining Figs. 3-1 and 3-2 into Fig. 3-3, we see that as long as Widget A's cost *relative to* B in terms of capacity utilization is less than its profitability (again *relative to* B), it "pays" our management to substitute A for B in the production process. Or graphically, as long as the slope of the production possibility curve differs from the slope of the equal profitability curve, the firm can move along its production possibilities frontier in the direction indicated by the arrow to higher profitability levels. Conversely, of course, as soon as Widget A's *resource cost* relative to B becomes less than its *profitability* relative to B, it "pays" management to move back along the production possibilities frontier, substituting B for A in its product mix until an optimal output combination is obtained—in the present instance by producing 286 and 145 units of Widgets A and B, respectively.

Notice that an optimal solution for the hypothetical resource allocation problem has occurred at a *corner* of the firm's production possibilities frontier, or opportunity set. A basic theorem (indeed, *the* basic theorem) of linear programming assures us that such a result is not at all coincidental but is assured by the linearity (i.e., the straight line character) of both the firm's objective function (Eq. 3-1) and its production possibilities frontier (Eqs. 3-2 through 3-5. A great many powerful mathematical arguments can be mustered to prove this perhaps surprising conclusion. For our purposes, however, such arguments are unnecessary. Intuition, combined with geometrical solutions such as Fig. 3-3 and any garden variety economist's marginalist notions, suffice to guarantee the theorem's credibility. Graphically, we can see that as long as an *effective* capacity constraint (i.e., one that forms a segment of the heavy "production possibilities frontier") crosses successive equal profit curves, profitability can be increased by moving along the frontier, one way or the other. An optimum, then, can occur only where either of these curves changes slope. The family of equal profit curves defined by Eq. 3-1 in a linear programming problem, clearly, will be constant throughout. Linearity also guarantees that each *segment* of our firm's production possibilities frontier has constant *slope*. The only point at which either curve can change slope, then, is at a *corner* where an additional capacity restriction becomes effective, causing an abrupt change in the rate at which one product's resource cost can be traded off against another's.

It should be apparent from Fig. 3-3 that, given our firm's production possibilities, its optimal product mix will depend not on the *absolute* profitability of either product but only on their *relative* costs and profitabilities. Should each good's operating profit margin be cut in half, for example, relative profitabilities and, hence, the slope of equal profit curves would be unaffected, as would the resulting optimal product mix. The only difference would be a substantial decrease in the amount of money carried by the firm to the bank each day. This difference, while perhaps enormous to most individuals (and to a great many businesses as well) is irrelevant to either a smart mathematician or a dumb computer whose purpose is to optimize a solution for a linear programming problem; for both know that, given the firm's opportunity set, its position always can be improved by trading one product for another until *relative* benefits no longer exceed *relative* resource costs at the margin.

Should our firm's profit on Widget B *alone* be reduced to $200 per unit, however, the change in *relative* profitability would drastically affect the firm's optimal product mix; for Widget A's *profit* relative to B now would exceed its *cost* relative to B in terms of *both* stamping and assembling resource costs. Geometrically, the new family of equal profit curves corresponding to profit margins of $300 and $200 on Widgets A and B is illustrated in Fig. 3-4. Widget B, clearly, disappears from the firm's optimal mix altogether. Indeed, in the absence of our supposedly trivial, non-negativity "programming constraints," the firm would be delighted to produce even fewer than zero units of the now-dominated product—if by so doing

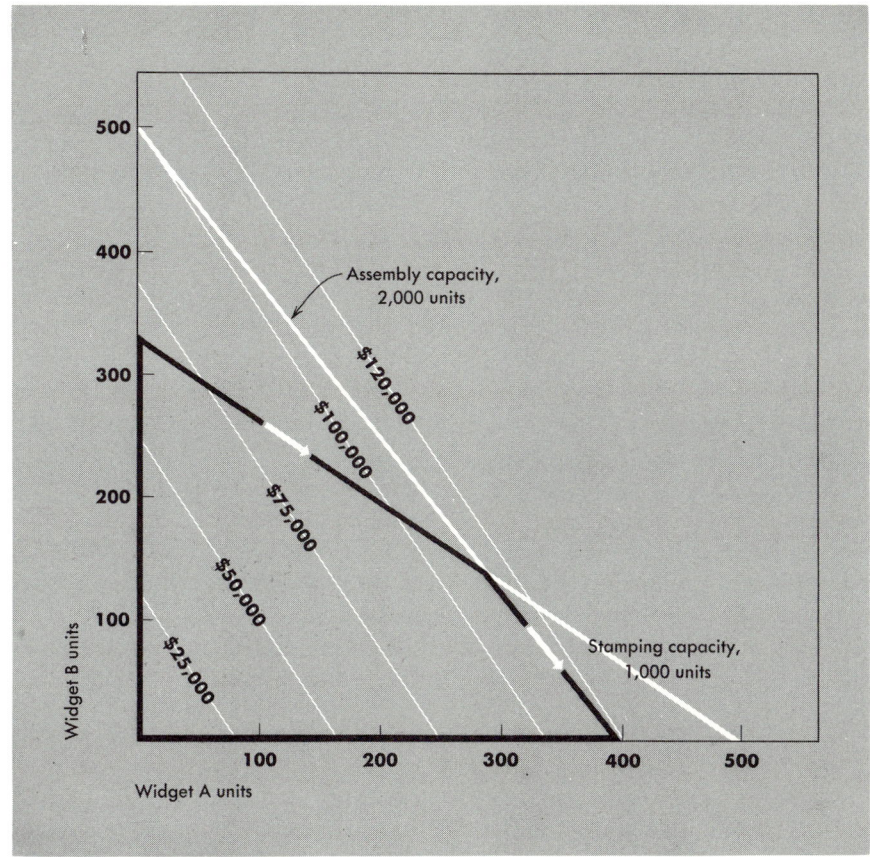

FIG. 3-4 Graphical solution, revised optimal product mix.

it could continue to increase its output of the dominant good at the terms of trade implied by its effective resource limitation; i.e., the firm would be willing to buy Widget B's at $200 per unit were it possible to transform them into additional units of assembly capacity, and thereby into additional production of A's (at the 4/5:A/B ratio implicit in the assembly capacity segment of the production possibilities frontier).

In a few cases, negative outputs are in fact conceivable. Debt, for example, may be thought of as equivalent to a negative cash balance. So also may "short sales" in various financial markets (such as those for stocks, bonds, and certain commodities) be considered equivalent to negative nonfinancial products. In general, however, the *programming constraints* that restrict production possibilities to non-negative output levels provide not only mathematical convenience for insuring the existence of a meaningful solution but also a realistic description of the options actually available to a manufacturing, or other nonfinancial, enterprise.

MATHEMATICAL PROGRAMMING AND THE DERIVATION OF SHADOW PRICES

The information obtainable from a linear programming problem does not end with its solution. Our hypothetical management, of course, will be happy to learn that for $300 and $360 operating profit margins, $\alpha = 286$ units of Widget A and $\beta = 145$ units of Widget B will constitute an optimal product mix, returning $138,000 in operating profit per year. And secure though they may be in the thought that this product mix is not only very good but actually is optimal under *existing* conditions, it is entirely possible that insight into the value of *altering* these conditions may be of even greater managerial significance than the solution itself. Linear programming, frequently, can provide such insight.

Consider again, for example, a solution to our hypothetical production problem such as that outlined at the end of the last section. Recall that by dropping the profit per unit on Widget B to $200 while A remains at $300 we found that it no longer pays to produce B's ($\alpha = 400$, $\beta = 0$; summarized in Fig. 3-4). Thus, by a change in the price structure Widget B was eliminated from production altogether. In this (or in fact, many other circumstances as well) management could well want to know, for example, how much would it be worth to expand *either* stamping *or* assembly capacities? In short, how would a *change* or modification in the resource limitations under which our company operates affect its attainable, operating cash flow?

In this case, where only one final product is produced and only one effective resource limitation exists, very little thought is required to establish either the firm's production possibilities or its attainable operating revenues. The reason, of course, is that excess stamping capacity already exists (one hundred units to be exact, as seen in Fig. 3-4). As any economist knows, and intuition in this case readily affirms, a resource already in excess supply has zero *marginal* revenue productivity and, therefore, no *marginal* value to the firm. Very little thought also is required in so simple an environment to calculate the marginal revenue productivity and, therefore, the marginal value to the firm of additions to assembly capacity, its "scarce" resource. As the operating profit margin on Widget A is presumed to be $300, and each additional unit of assembly capacity can support one-fifth of a unit of A production, the marginal revenue productivity, opportunity cost, shadow price, or simply the "marginal value available to the company from an extra unit of assembly capacity" is easily seen to be $300/5 = $60 per unit.

Under our initial price structure, however, where both stamping and assembly capacities constitute effective resource limitations (Fig. 3-3), these marginal revenue productivity figures, or shadow prices, are more difficult to compute. Recalling that the stamping capacity of our hypothetical firm was 1,000 units, we might consider what it would be worth to us to expand that capacity, say by the minimum increment of one from 1,000 to 1,001 units. Specifically, what effect would such a marginal increase have on the firm's attainable production and, accordingly, on its cash flow? [2]

One procedure for answering these questions would be to replace the original problem's stamping capacity limitation by 1,001 units and repeat the problem's entire solution. Similarly, for assembly capacity, a new solution employing 2,001 rather than 2,000 units of assembly capacity could be obtained and compared to the original solution to ascertain the marginal increase in operating profit. Were one to perform both these calculations independently, increases in operating profit approximating $86/year per unit of stamping capacity and $26/year per unit of assembly capacity would be discovered. In practice so laborious a method of evaluating each scarce resource's marginal revenue productivity, or shadow price, is unnecessary. Actually, by use of some quite ingenious but nevertheless simple to apply mathematics, the shadow prices can be obtained more or less as a by-product of the problem's direct solution. It is beyond our task here to prove the so-called duality theorem on which these shadow price determinations are made. For present purposes it will have to suffice to note that the shadow price concept is built into two very fundamental properties of the programming approach. The first, emphasized earlier, is that a resource already in excess supply is equivalent to a "free good." The second pertains to a fundamental "symmetry" required of all linear programming solutions: that all value obtainable from an *optimal* product mix be fully (exactly) imputed to a firm's *scarce* resources. The prices that make that imputation are the shadow prices set equal to marginal revenue productivity.

We can illustrate this numerically in the two cases already discussed. Observe that for our single-product solution, the total value of Widget A's produced is equal to $300 (400) = $120,000; this must be fully imputed to the firm's one scarce resource, assembly capacity. This imputation can be made by assigning a shadow price of $60 to each of the 2,000 units of assembly capacity for $60 × 2,000 = $120,000. For our multi-product, multi-resource solution the combined output values were $300 × (286 units) + $360 × (145 units) = $138,000. This total value will be fully imputed to the underlying resources, stamping capacity and assembly capacity, by assigning shadow prices of $86 and $26 respectively; then $86 (1,000) + $26 (2,000) = $138,000 in combined assembly and stamping capacity resource values.

The two characteristics on which shadow prices are based also make reasonably good economic sense. As noted, it seems quite proper to impute zero value to those resources whose quantity can be varied without in any way affecting the firm's production possibilities. Such resources are obviously in superfluous abundance and can be logically regarded as free. Not quite so

---

[2] This is the same as asking how steep is the gradient in Fig. 3-4 between successive equal profit curves as one moves in a direction perpendicular to the firm's "stamping capacity" frontier.

obvious, perhaps, is the notion that *all* values actually created can, in fact, be imputed to the firm's "scarce" resources, in accordance with their "marginal revenue productivities." But there is, at least, a certain intuitive appeal in saying that the resources that create certain values must in some sense share those values. As noted, the marginal revenue productivity or shadow price approach also defines these shares in a linear programming problem in such a way that the allocation is complete. A bookkeeping, as well as simple logical, neatness accrues to having the sum of the resource shares equal the total value of all the products produced and vice versa.

By developing a whole array of relatively sophisticated mathematical tools, it would be possible to delve beneath the surface of these properties and bind the concept of shadow price, or imputed resource value, more tightly to the core of the economist's opportunity cost concept. One could also develop and point out a number of properties specific to linear programming alone, as distinct from the wider class of mathematical programming tools to which it belongs. For now, however, these more intuitive presentations of this highly useful tool, the shadow price, will have to suffice. We will, though, return subsequently to two other applications of the shadow price concept which may help to further elucidate the concept.

PROCESS FORMULATIONS OF MATHEMATICAL PROGRAMMING

Our view of almost any problem (and its solution) generally is conditioned to a considerable extent by our choice of mathematical, graphical, or verbal constructs for its formulation and representation. We all are, to a greater or lesser extent, captives of images that are our own creations and are limited in our ability to more fully understand particular problems by our ability to view them from sufficiently different perspectives. By formulating our linear programming model graphically in terms of "products," we are able to appreciate the essential tradeoffs imposed by resource limitations on our choice of an optimal "product" mix. It is more difficult from such a perspective, however, to visualize the parallel "resource," or "factor" allocation, or tradeoff that simultaneously underlies such an optimum. It is instructive, therefore, to reformulate our simple, illustrative problem in terms of "resources" rather than "products," to focus attention on the economic *processes* by which physical resources are transformed into tangible products, and through them into operating cash flows for the firm.

Let us begin by defining the concept of an economic or production process, not in terms of a sequence of acts—such as: first, stamp out the pieces; second, bolt them together; and third, paint them blue—but in terms of the resource needs per unit of output required by such a sequence. For our hypothetical illustration, then, *any* way of producing a good that requires the *same* quantity of stamping and assembling capacities per unit of output will be said to constitute the same production "process."

From Eqs. 3-2 and 3-3 above, it is clear that very simple and rigid processes indeed are specified for our firm's production of Widget A (automobiles) and Widget B (buses). Specifically, we can see that 2 units of stamping capacity and 5 units of assembly capacity, neither more nor less, are required to produce a single A per unit of time. We are further assured that these *unit factor intensities* do not depend in any way on the numbers of autos or buses produced. Measuring units of assembly and stamping capacities along Fig. 3-5's horizontal and vertical axes, respectively (instead of outputs of A and B as before), we can plot the *total resource needs* for any particular level of automobile output as a single point. Five hundred units of assembly capacity and 200 units of stamping capacity, for example, are required to support 100 units of annual automobile production. Similarly, 1,000 units of assembly and 400 units of stamping capacities are required to produce 200 automobiles; while 2,000 and 800 units of assembly and stamping capacities, respectively, are needed to support a 400 unit annual output rate. Connecting these points by 2 simple, straight lines to the origin in Fig. 3-5 to create an "automobile production process ray," we can immediately summarize the resource needs implied by any level of output whatever for the automobile production "process" in our hypothetical problem.

By an identical procedure, we can derive from the fact that *exactly* 3 units of stamping capacity and 4 units of assembly capacity are required to

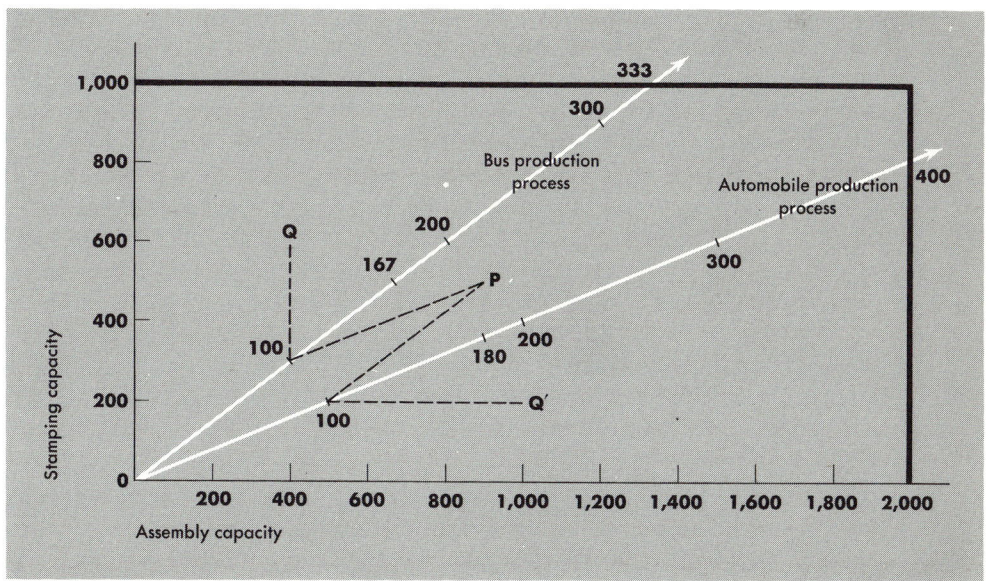

FIG. 3-5 Production processes in resources space.

produce a single bus, that 300 and 400 units of stamping and assembly capacities are needed to produce 100 buses; 600 and 800 units, respectively, to produce 200 buses, etc., and summarize the whole array of possible input-output combinations by Fig. 3-5's upper straight line, or production process ray, for bus production.

Two very strong linearity assumptions, clearly, are embodied in such a representation. The first and easiest to swallow, perhaps, is that proportionate changes in *all* factor inputs will lead to identical proportionate changes in output; or in classical economic jargon, that neither increasing nor decreasing but *constant* returns to scale are assumed to exist. The second, that factors of production can be used only in fixed proportions, however, will cause most students of traditional economics, including those who have just finished the preceding chapters, to quiver; for theory and intuition alike assure us that labor and capital, or stamping and assembly facilities, *can* be substituted for one another at the margin. Even in highly automated assembly line operations, for example, one worker equipped with power tools may be able to replace two or three workers having only hand tools at their disposal. So also may our firm, by improving the quality control standards applied to its stamping operation, reduce assembly capacity needs per unit of output, etc.

Both these statements, though true, are not necessarily inconsistent with our use of *specific* input-output combinations to define *specific* production processes. They simply point out the desirability, and in many cases the importance, of introducing *different* economic or technological processes to describe different ways of making the same product, a practice that greatly increases the operational flexibility of linear programming. Algebraically, such a modification would be equivalent to adding an additional variable to each of the basic equations of a linear programming problem for each new "process" introduced (as well as an extra non-negativity or "programming" restriction). Geometrically, an additional linear process can be represented simply as another process ray in a diagram such as Fig. 3-5.

There is, in theory, no limit to the number of processes that can be handled in this fashion. Given the ability of large scale digital computers to solve in a very few minutes linear programming problems that contain literally hundreds of variables (or processes) and capacity restrictions, there also are relatively few practical limitations to the flexibility that can be obtained in such a manner. Returning for the moment to our original two-inputs in precisely fixed proportions, it is clear that increases in one not accompanied by increases in the other will necessarily be wasted. Taking Q in Fig. 3-5 as an example, an ability to stamp out sufficient parts for 200 buses per year cannot insure their production if assembly facilities permit only 100 units to be completed. The excess stamping capacity represented by such a factor combination must either lie idle or be used to fill warehouses with unassembled parts. Conversely, a factor combination such as Q', that provides an ability to assemble twice as many automobile parts as the firm's stamping facilities can provide, is of little analytical (or practical) value. Unless "processes" exist which have greater "assembly intensities" than our firm's automobiles, or greater "stamping intensities" than its buses, it is clear that no factor combination lying outside Fig. 3-5's "process fan" can be consistent with the full utilization of available resources—for in either case some, or at least one, process must lie idle; or to say the same thing differently, the same quantity of output could have been produced with a lesser quantity of at least one factor input.

It does not follow, however, that facor combinations lying within this "fan" (but not on either process ray) also must involve unused resources; for by *combining processes* having different factor intensities, one may obtain any intermediate (composite) resource mix. Take the 900 units of assembly capacity and 500 units of stamping capacity represented by point P in Fig. 3-5 as an example. Such a combination, clearly, could result from the combination of appropriate assembly and stamping capacities from 100 units each of automobile and bus manufacturing "processes." It may be useful to verify this assertion numerically, or if one prefers, graphically, by *adding* a vector having one process' resource intensity (i.e., its slope) to the other process ray, and sliding the former along the latter until the point in question is intersected (as by the dotted lines through P in Fig. 3-5). Relying on an elementary theorem of plane geometry regarding the equality of opposing sides for parellelograms, one can read off the product mix corresponding to any attainable resource mix directly from the new vectors' intersections with the original process rays. By experimenting a bit with overall product and resource combinations, one's ability to vary resource intensities by varying product or "process" mixes, and vice versa—and therefore, the *equivalence* of "product" and "resource" allocation problems—should become clear.

Still missing, of course, is information about the relative desirability, or profitability, of obtaining any particular resource or product mix. However, for each available process one can determine and plot the number of units of output and, therefore, the resource combinations required to yield any specified level of operating revenues per year. Recalling that automobiles and buses are here assumed to yield $300 and $360 of such revenues in unit operating profits, respectively, it is clear that *either* 100 automobiles *or* 83 buses per year can produce a total annual operating profit of $30,000. It also must be true, then, that a combination of $100/2 = 50$ automobiles and $83/2 = 42$ buses (each of which offers $15,000 by itself) together must yield $30,000, as will any other point on the straight-line $30,000 equal profit curve shown in Fig. 3-6. Identical exercises, of course, can with equal ease produce the $60,000, $90,000, $120,000 and $138,000 equal profit curves illustrated in the diagram.

Presented in this fashion, our earlier excursion into imputed values or shadow prices for factors of production begins to take on greater intuitive meaning. For here, monetary "values" are attached graphically not to final products but to the resource or factor inputs that go into their manufacture. By moving along an equal profit curve, the rate at which one factor must be substituted for another at the margin to maintain any given level of operating profit (as changes in product mix yield effective changes in factor composition) can be measured directly. From our $60,000 constant profit curve, for example, 100 additional units of stamping capacity are sufficient to compensate for the 333 unit reduction in assembly capacity involved in a transfer of resources from automobile to bus manufacturing processes. Identical 3⅓ to 1 marginal tradeoffs, of course, could be obtained from any other pair of "equal profit" combinations. Factor prices (or values) also may be derived by moving along process rays to different profit levels. Note from the auto process ray that 500 extra units of assembly capacity together with 200 units of stamping capacity always are able to add $30,000 to our firm's annual profits, and that 333 additional units of assembly and 250 units of stamping capacity devoted to the firm's bus manufacturing operation adds an identical $30,000 amount to operating cash flow. Defining shadow prices or imputed values for additional units of assembly and stamping capacities, as V_a and V_s respectively, we may summarize these relationships as

$$500\ V_a + 200\ V_s = \$30,000 \quad \text{(for automobiles)}$$
$$333\ V_a + 250\ V_s = \$30,000 \quad \text{(for buses)}$$

and solve them to obtain shadow prices

$$V_a = \$25.7$$
$$V_s = \$85.7$$

which are the same as those described earlier.

Once financial and technological information are combined, as in Fig. 3-6, our problem's formal solution for an *optimal* resource allocation is virtually obvious. The input combination utilizing all 2,000 available units of assembly and 1,000 units of stamping capacity to produce 286 automobiles and 143 buses per year, attains the maximum $138,000 annual operating profit available to our firm. We are, of course, happy that this solution corresponds to that originally obtained when dealing in terms of products. Our purpose in repeating it here, however, is not to demonstrate its mathematical invariance but rather is to develop and reinforce some of the fundamental economic properties that lurk beneath the formal structure of any mathematical programming problem.

The first of these, mentioned earlier, is the enormous operational flexibility obtainable within a programming format through the liberal definition and use of alternative economic or technological "processes."

Second is the effective substitutability of factor inputs for one another through variations in product, or process, mix.

Third is the further intuitive development of imputed resource values or shadow prices; a demonstration that always has been one of mathematical

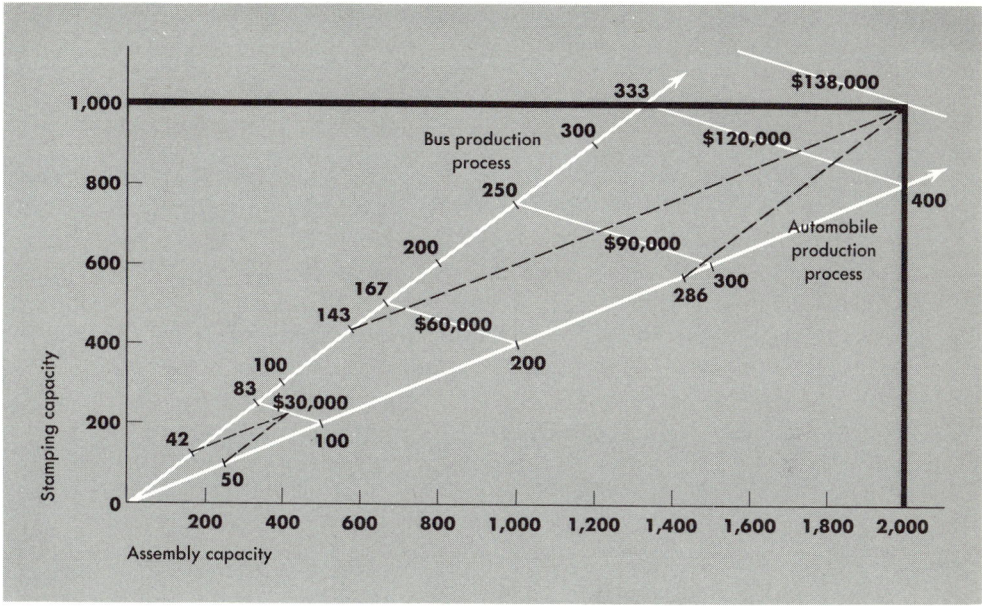

FIG. 3-6 Graphical solution, optimal resource allocation.

programming's greatest contributions to either economic or operations analysis.

And finally, by reformulating even very simple optimization problems such as the one developed here, the essential identity of resource and product allocation problems can be illustrated with extra force and clarity.

GENERALIZATIONS AND FURTHER APPLICATIONS

By developing mathematical programming to this point through a highly restrictive, two dimensional linear programming problem, there is some danger that one may think of these methods as academic toys rather than operational tools. Before leaving this chapter, therefore, it may be worthwhile to eliminate any such misconception. Mathematical programming is hardly a toy. Linear programming problems containing hundreds of variables and capacity restrictions are solved routinely and inexpensively every day by practical persons in government and industry facing practical, resource allocation problems. Brute computational power—attributable jointly to high speed computers and efficient numerical procedures—undoubtedly is one source of the method's popularity. Increased flexibility through an ability to handle nonlinear relationships, or discrete (accept or reject) solutions, however, also adds to programming's operational potential, as some examples may help to illustrate.

Nonlinear Returns

Suppose a firm faces a production problem identical in every respect to that belabored earlier *except that* declining rather than constant returns to scale are anticipated. Reasons for such an occurrence are easily imagined—indeed, much more easily than the constant returns assumption underlying our original formulation. Whatever its source (increasing costs or decreasing prices) let us assume that operating profit margins for automobiles and buses, respectively, can be defined not by the pair of constants,

$$\pi_a = \$300 \quad \text{for automobiles}$$
$$\pi_\beta = \$360 \quad \text{for buses}$$

assumed earlier (and drawn as horizontal straight lines in Fig. 3-7), but by the figure's downward sloping output-profit curves, whose values may be approximated either by (dotted) step functions or, algebraically, by simple linear relationships,

$$\pi_a = 400 - .4a \quad \text{for automobiles}$$
$$\pi_\beta = 450 - .6\beta \quad \text{for buses}$$

when a and β represent quantities of autos and buses produced, as before.

At least two ways of incorporating this type of *nonlinear* relationship into an analysis are commonly employed. The first and most accurate is, simply, to incorporate each product's declining profit margin directly into the algebraic expression for our problem's objective function, i.e., replace the problem's original *linear* objective function

$$\pi = \$300a + \$360\beta$$

by

$$\pi = \$(400 - .4a)\, a + \$(450 - .6\beta)\, \beta$$

which, on simplification, becomes a *quadratic* expression for total operating profit per year. Assuming capacity limitations to remain unchanged, the entire problem can be reformulated as

Maximize

$$\pi = \$400a - \$.4a^2 + \$450\beta - \$.6\beta^2 \qquad \text{(Eq. 3-1)}$$

Subject to the original set of linear restrictions,

$$2\alpha + 3\beta \leq 1{,}000 \quad \text{stamping capacity limitation} \quad \text{(Eq. 3-2)}$$

$$5\alpha + 4\beta \leq 2{,}000 \quad \text{assembly capacity limitations} \quad \text{(Eq. 3-3)}$$

and

$$\alpha \geq 0 \quad \text{(Eq. 3-4)}$$

non-negativity, or programming constraints

$$\beta \geq 0 \quad \text{(Eq. 3-5)}$$

Conceptually, almost nothing has changed. Our objective, presumably, continues to be a profit maximizing set of *attainable* resource and product combinations; where attainability, as before, is defined through Eqs. 3-2 through 3-5. Changing the problem's objective function from linear to quadratic, of course, introduces computational problems; for the nonlinear equal profit curves so defined (in product and resource spaces) no longer can be guaranteed to produce strictly corner solutions. These problems, however, are well within *quadratic programming's* "state of the art," and need not detain us here. It is sufficient to note at this point that nonlinear mathematical programming techniques permit important generalizations of the many "constant return" assumptions that often restrict linear programming's credibility.

Such generalizations, however, may be purchased at considerable cost in terms of computational speed; for one's ability to "hop" from corner to corner on an opportunity set of a "linear" programming problem (without searching the area in between for an optimum) is one of the method's greatest practical aids for simplifying calculations.

In some cases, therefore, one may attempt to "stretch" a linear pro-

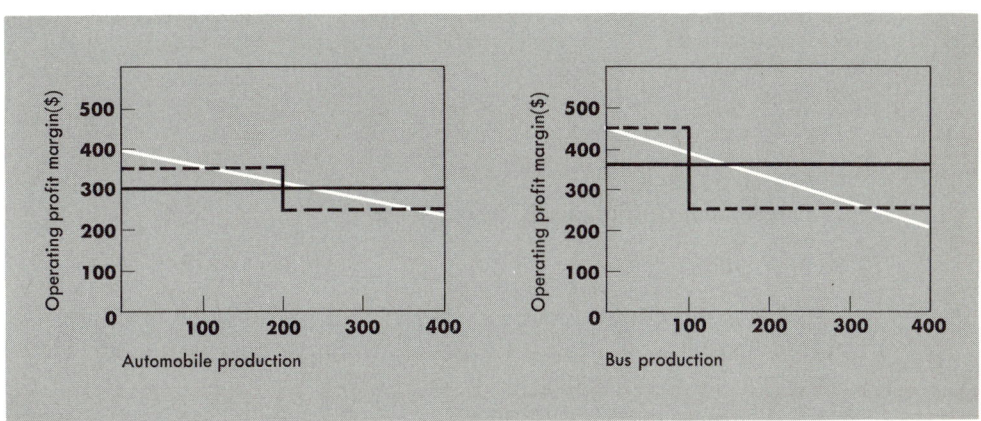

FIG. 3-7 Decreasing returns to scale, alternative representations.

gramming format to "approximate" a nonlinear problem's structure and solution. Consider the dotted line, piecewise approximation for automobile and bus operating profit margins in Fig. 3-7. One could, if he wished, consider automobiles and buses sold at different prices to be, simply, different products whose resource needs happen to be the same, i.e., one could define a_1 as units of automobile output yielding $350 operating profits, a_2 as automobiles yielding only $250 operating profits, both of which require 2 units of stamping and 5 units of assembly capacity to produce. Similarly, β_1 could be introduced as a process whose operating profit margin is $450, β_2 as a separate process whose profit is $250; yet both require 3 and 4 units of stamping and assembly capacities per unit of output.

It should be clear, however, that barring limits on our ability to produce a_1 and β_1, products a_2 and β_2 never would enter a sensible firm's product mix; for both consume the same scarce resources yet yield lower returns per unit of output. It would be silly, for example, to produce a_2 instead of a_1, or β_2 instead of β_1 *if the converse were possible.* The existence of downward sloping demand curves, or decreasing returns to scale, however, reflects the fact that unlimited quantities of each product *cannot* be sold at premium prices. Specifically, Fig. 3-7 explicitly introduces a "step" (from $350 to $250) in automobile operating profit margins, and another (from $450 to $250) in bus profitability at 100 units. Adding these limitations as "stepwise restrictions" to our linear programming format, we may reformulate the entire problem as

maximize
$$\$350\, a_1 + \$250\, a_2 + \$450\, \beta_1 + \$250\, \beta_2 \quad \text{(Eq. 3-1)}$$

subject to an expanded set of restrictions, on stamping and assembly capacity limitations

$$2(a_1 + a_2) + 3(\beta_1 + \beta_2) \leq 1{,}000 \quad \text{(Eq. 3-2)}$$
$$5(a_1 + a_2) + 4(\beta_1 + \beta_2) \leq 2{,}000 \quad \text{(Eq. 3-3)}$$

stepwise output restrictions,

$$a_1 \leq 200 \quad \text{(Eq. 3-4)}$$
$$\beta_1 \leq 100 \quad \text{(Eq. 3-5)}$$

and conventional "programing" restrictions

$$a_1, a_2, \beta_1, \beta_2, \geq 0 \quad \text{(Eqs. 3-6 through 3-9)}$$

Several worthwhile points may be illustrated by this exercise. The first is the flexibility with which additional "processes" may be used to increase a mathematical programming problem's viability. Second is the wide range of side conditions—beyond simple capacity and non-negativity restrictions—that can be built into such problems. And third, although it has not yet been brought out, is the relative insensitivity of many solutions to such refinements. Along this line we may note that neither of the two preceding modifications has changed our problem's solution in any way. Two hundred and eighty-six automobiles and 143 buses continue to constitute an optimal product mix for our hypothetical firm.

Integer Solutions

One problem that often is not trivial, however, is the assumed divisibility of inputs and outputs built into conventional programming models, both linear and nonlinear. We are able to live quite comfortably with such an assumption in our automobile-bus manufacturing example—despite the fact that its precise solution calls not for the production of 286 and 143 autos and buses, but 286.666 and 143.333 respective units of output. We know of course that ⅓ of an automobile and ⅔ of a bus are difficult to market; but we are not unduly concerned by so minor a discrepancy between theoretical and practical optima.

For some purposes, however, fractional solutions simply cannot be tolerated. A paper company attempting to optimize locations for multi-million dollar paper machines cannot live with a linear programming model whose solution dictates the construction of 1.730 machines at Klamath, Oregon, .472 machines near Bonner, Montana, .136 at Bogalusa, Lousiana, and 2.148 near Millinocket, Maine. Such machines stand several stories tall, cost millions of dollars, and like most highly automated facilities, are quite indivisible.

Similarly, a decision maker faced with a choice between mutually exclusive ways of doing the same thing, must choose (at most) one candidate project and reject all the others. He cannot, for example, decide to build ½ of a hydroelectric power station at point Z, and another ½ two miles downstream, at point W. Further examples involving processes whose only feasible levels of output are zero (if the process is rejected altogether) or unity (if accepted) can be manufactured *ad infinitum*. For our purposes, however, it is sufficient to point out that such problems *do* exist, and that computing algorithms capable of dealing with them—called *integer programming* methods —also have been developed and are available today to applied researchers. To avoid overselling the product, however, one should be cautioned that integer programming methods involve the creation of *very large numbers of* artificial variables (or processes) and restrictions. As a result, even fairly modest integer programming problems often tend to become computationally expensive (or even unmanageable), placing a premium on the development of approximate solutions for such problems.[3]

---

[3] An example of this is the algorithm applied by Weingartner to the Lorrie-Savage multiple period planning problem discussed in Chapter Four of this volume; see H. Martin Weingartner, *Mathematical Programming and the Analysis of Capital Budgeting Problems* (Englewood Cliffs, N.J.: Prentice-Hall, Inc., 1963).

During its short history, mathematical programming has emerged from its academic cocoon into a fully operational, and at times even beautiful, butterfly. To an economist this beauty may emanate from the applicability of basic marginal concepts to significant, operational resource allocation problems. To an entrepreneur, the method's beauty often may be measured quite tangibly, in the Net Worth column of his balance sheet. To a planner in government, or at the divisional level of large, decentralized corporations, mathematical programming's beauty may derive from its applicability to cost minimizing resource combinations; or from a shadow price's ability to *impute* opportunity costs to externally imposed resource limitations—such as divisional or agency budgets.

The moral to be drawn from these observations, however, is that mathematical programming, or any other analytic tool that combines powerful computational capabilities with sound economic principles, can be expected to play a significant role in modern managerial economics.

Capital Budgeting

CHAPTER FOUR

THE PRESENT VALUE CRITERION

The marginal concepts developed and illustrated in the previous chapters also can be applied to what is perhaps the most basic of all managerial choices, the firm's capital expenditures or capital budgeting decisions. Capital budgeting, essentially, determines the direction in which a firm progresses (or retrogresses) over time. It is the analytical basis for decisions to produce new products or establish new markets, to substitute one technology or production process for another, to expand production or create new plants, to merge with sources of supply or new channels for distribution, to diversify through the acquisition of firms in new fields of activity, and so forth, over all decisions that involve the commitment of *current* sums of money to obtain *future* benefits or returns.

Such commitments of funds are undertaken only in the expectation of future gains, or returns larger than the amounts currently committed. Any sensible man places a higher value on a dollar today than a dollar tomorrow, or a year from now. This is true, if for no other reason, because a dollar invested today in earning assets (including an insured savings account in the local bank) can earn *interest* and, as a result, can be worth more than a dollar tomorrow. For example, if the interest received on an investment were 10 percent, one dollar lent or otherwise invested today would accumulate to one dollar and 10 cents, one year from now; similarly, if interest were 5 percent, one dollar and 5 cents could be obtained a year from now on every dollar invested today. Or more generally, defining r as the rate of interest expressed as a "fractional return on invested funds per period of time," $(1 + r)$

47

dollars can be obtained per dollar invested today at the end of a single period of time.

Conversely, one dollar promised in payment one year from now ordinarily is deemed to be worth less than a dollar today, or more specifically to have a *present value* of only

$$V = \frac{1}{(1+r)}.$$

This follows because the "alternative opportunity" always exists of investing $1/(1+r)$ current dollars at the rate of return r. Such an investment would return $\left[\frac{1}{(1+r)}\right] \times (1+r) = \$1.00$ by the end of the year. Numerically, then, 95 cents is said to be the present value (at a 5 percent rate of interest, r) of $1.00 a year from now because, invested at 5 percent, 95 cents in present dollars would be worth $0.95 \times (\$1.05) = \$1.00$ by the end of the year.

Similarly, a current dollar invested in assets (or held in a savings account), earning r percent per year for two years, would be worth its $(1+r)$ value at the end of the first year *times* the $(1+r)$ *earned on that amount* during the second year, or

$$(1+r)(1+r) = (1+r)^2.$$

Thus, as we have already seen, $0.95 invested for one year at a 5 percent rate of interest will be worth $1.00 by the end of the year. If this $1.00 then were reinvested to earn 5 percent for a second year, it would be worth $1.05 by the second year's end, since $\$1.00 \times \$1.05 = \$1.05$. These two calculations (for the first and second years) can be collapsed into one since all we are doing is multiplying the initial value (or present value) by $(1+r)$, or $1.05 on two successive occasions. So our calculation is simply

$$\$0.95 \, (1.05) \, (1.05) = .95 \, (1.05)^2 = \$1.05$$

There is, of course, no reason why we must stop with two years. We can continue for three, four, or n years. Any current investment value would accumulate to its own value multiplied by $(1+r)(1+r)\ldots(1+r) = (1+r)^t$ by the end of t years for any value of $t = 1, 2, \ldots, n$ whatever. Inversely, one dollar promised for payment at the end of t time periods (or years) can be said to have a *present value* of only

$$V = \frac{1}{(1+r)^t}.$$

Again, this holds true *because V* dollars available today for investment at the

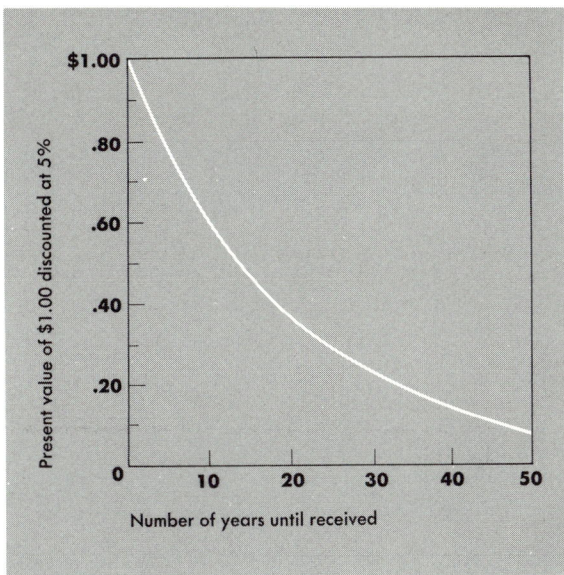

FIG. 4-1 Decline in present value with increase in number of years of discounting.

rate r could *exactly reproduce* the $1.00 payment promised t years hence. By the same token, the present value of any amount, say y_t dollars, available t years from now, could be written as

$$V = \frac{y_t}{(1+r)^t}.$$

In general, of course, the further into the future one expects to receive a given return, the less its present value will be; this is shown graphically by the relation between a single dollar's *present value* and the number of time periods until it becomes available at an $r = 5$ percent rate of interest in Fig. 4-1.[1]

The present value of a *sequence* of returns, say y_1 for the first year, y_2 for the second year, and so on through y_n for the nth year can be expressed in a number of ways. The most straightforward is, simply, as the *sum of the present values* of returns for *each* period of time. Thus, we can determine the present value, call it v_1, of the first year's return, y_1, by applying our present value formula, as

[1] For alternative development of this same topic elsewhere in this *Series*, see J. Duesenberry, *Money and Credit: Impact and Control,* 2nd edition, Chapters 5, 6.

$$v_1 = \frac{y_1}{(1+r)}.$$

For the second year this would be

$$v^2 = \frac{y_2}{(1+r)^2},$$

and on to the nth or final year, when

$$v_n = \frac{y_n}{(1+r)^n}.$$

We then can define the sum of all these present values for different years as V, which is the total present value of the entire stream of returns, $y_1, y_2, \ldots, y_n$. Thus

$$V = v_1 + v_2 + \ldots + v_n,$$

or, substituting,

$$V = \frac{y_1}{(1+r)} + \frac{y_2}{(1+r)^2} + \ldots + \frac{y_n}{(1+r)^n}. \quad \text{(Eq. 4-1)}$$

Standard tables for calculating the present value of a single future payment or level sequence of such payments for a wide range of discount rates r and future periods n can be found in Appendix A, Tables 1 and 2, respectively.

Before applying such a formula mechanically to obtain a particular asset's present value, one must of course estimate the cash flow y_t expected during each year or period of time. This may not be easy; in fact, it very often is the most difficult aspect of any realistic capital budgeting analysis. The complication is that the future consequences of any particular decision usually are known or perceived only with considerable uncertainty. We shall bypass this problem for the moment deferring its discussion until Chapter 5.

It also should be noted that only the *net* cash flow from an investment should be entered into present value calculations. In particular, any expenses associated with an asset's operation (or simply its holding) should be deducted from the period's gross revenues before discounting to determine a present value, V. Should the asset in question be a machine that produces widgets, for example, all expenses for operating the machine, maintaining it, providing associated materials, etc., must be deducted from each period's revenues from selling widgets, before entering the period's net cash flow y^t in Eq. 4-1's present value formula.

Given an asset's present value and costs, management's decision problem is perfectly simple, conceptually. An investment should be undertaken as long as "it is worth more than it costs," or more precisely, as long as "the present value of its returns is greater than the present value of its costs." To say the same thing differently, an investment should be undertaken as long as its present value *net of all costs*, or *net present value*, is greater than zero. Such an asset is, quite literally, worth more to the firm's owners than it costs to acquire. Should a firm wish to maximize its profits or net worth, then, any investment that is worth more than it costs ought to be acquired.

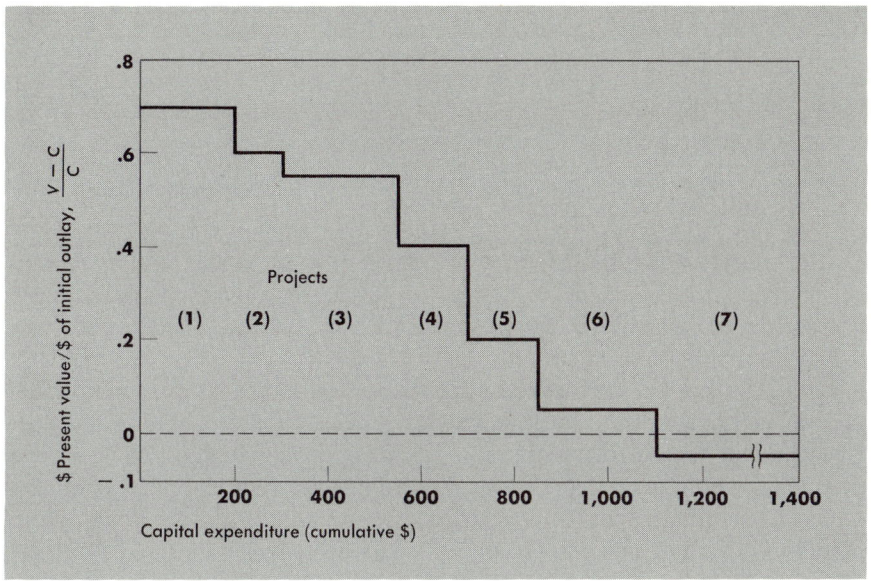

FIG. 4-2 An illustrative listing of capital investment projects by net present value per dollar of cost.

In actuality, this goal may not be achieved because of limitations on a firm's available investment capital. Defining V as an asset's present value, C as its original cost (and therefore $V - C$ as its *net* present value), projects ordinarily are ranked according to net present values *per dollar of initial cost,* as in Fig. 4-2, and accepted (or undertaken) until either the firm's capital budget has been exhausted or no further investments having positive net present values remain, whichever occurs first. By way of illustration, consider a firm whose seven most attractive investment opportunities are arrayed stepwise as in Fig. 4-2. If this firm arbitrarily limits itself to a $700 capital budget, only the first four of its projects, offering combined *net present values over and above capital costs* can be undertaken.

As long as the interest rate or cost of capital r used for discounting purposes accurately reflects the rate at which funds are available to the firm (in unlimited amounts) for such expenditures, any management that observes an arbitrary budget constraint and foregoes projects whose present values are greater than their costs (such as 5 and 6 in Fig. 4-2's example) behaves in a less than optimal fashion. Returning to marginal principles, such a management is, basically, refusing to undertake projects whose marginal revenues, properly discounted for futurity, are greater than their marginal costs. Conversely, a management that, through accident or design, accepts a project (such as 7 in Fig. 4-2) whose *net* present value is negative, reduces the value of the firm to its owners by paying more for the asset than it is worth—or literally, by transforming one type of asset, *cash*, into a *less valuable* physical asset.

ALTERNATIVE CRITERIA

The Payoff Period

Several alternatives to "discounted present value" are in reasonably common use by managers today for evaluating capital outlays. None of these is as satisfactory as net present value, but because of their wide use, their properties deserve attention.

One of these is the so-called payback period. Payback, most simply defined, is the number of years required for a project's net operating revenues to accumulate to the total cost of its original capital outlay. Thus, if one were to consider a project costing $100, yielding level returns of $25 annually, net of all operating expenses, its payback period would be four years; more generally, if annual net returns of y dollars were generated by a project costing C dollars to procure and install, C/y would constitute the project's payback period. Used as a criterion for choosing between alternative investment opportunities, projects having quick payoffs are preferred to those whose immediate cash flows per dollar of initial outlay are more sparse—and therefore take longer to recover initial costs.[2]

As a criterion for capital budgeting in the absence of uncertainty, payback is virtually indefensible—as it accounts in only the most haphazard of ways for the fact that a dollar today and a dollar tomorrow will be worth quite different amounts to a sensible investor. An example or two may help to illustrate. Consider first a pair of projects, each costing $100; assume that one returns $10 during the first year and $90 during the second year of operation, while the other returns $90 during the first and $10 during the second year. Let us further assume that each project returns the same, unspecified amount X during all subsequent years of its life. Each, clearly, has a two-year payback period and, accordingly, would be considered equally valuable (and quite attractive) under a payback criterion. From our earlier discussion, however, it is clear that the two projects' present values *could not be the same,* for one offers the extra $80 during the *first* year of its life, while the other does so only during the *second* year. By failing to distinguish between the *timing* of cash payments within a project's payoff period, payback misses an important element in the time value of money.

Even more potentially damaging, however, is the fact that payback

---

[2] For further discussion of payback and other investment criteria, see M. J. Gordon, "The Payoff Period and the Rate of Profit," and other articles compiled by E. Solomon, ed., in *The Management of Corporate Capital* (New York: Free Press of Glencoe, 1959).

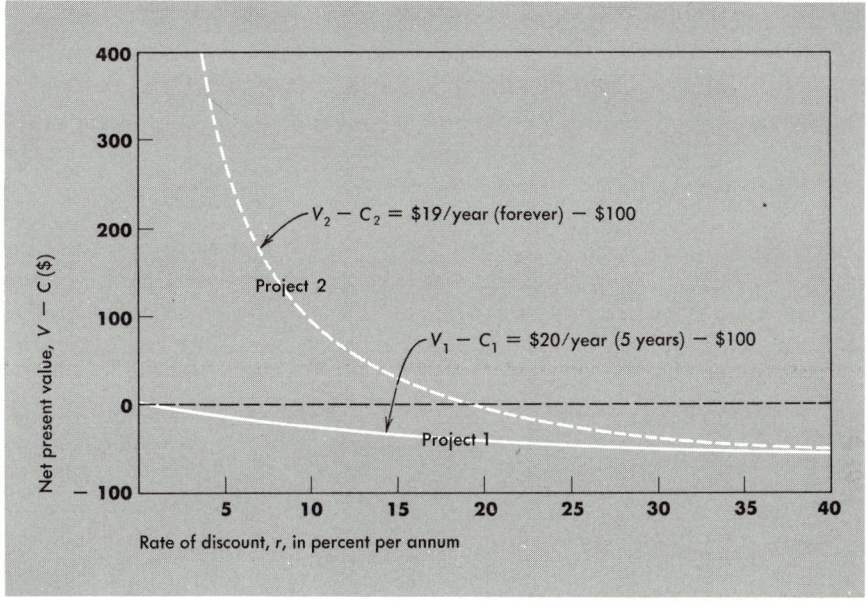

FIG. 4-3 A comparison of two projects ranking differently on net present value and payout criteria.

entirely ignores cash payments (such as the unspecified X in our example) that occur *after* a project's original capital expenditure has been recovered. Such payments could be the same or different between our two projects; they could be either very large or very small; they could even be *negative* without entering into payback calculations in any way. Consider, for example, a second pair of illustrative projects, each costing $100 as before, the first of which returns $20 per year for five years and *nothing thereafter,* while the other returns $19 per year *forever.* The first, clearly, has a payback period of five years and the second a payback of 5.26 years. Using payback as a measure of project desirability, then, the first is the superior of the two projects. Comparing present values over a wide range of possible interest rates in Fig. 4-3, however, it is clear that there is *no* positive interest rate whatever at which the first project would be more valuable to an investor than the second and, moreover, that there is no positive (non zero) interest rate at which the first project would even be desirable in an absolute sense, as its net present value *always* is negative. The second project, returning $19 per year in perpetuity, on the other hand, would be worth more than its cost (or have a positive net present value) for any rate of interest, or cost of capital less than 19 percent per annum.

Payback's debilitating limitations in these, as in so many other comparative applications, then, are: first, its inability to distinguish between the timing of payments occurring *within* a project's payoff period; and second, its inability to incorporate in any way cash flows that occur *beyond* the payback period.

These criticisms may appear to be directed at a "straw man," however, for payback seldom is justified today as a criterion for project evaluation in the absence of a great deal of risk or uncertainty about the capital expenditure's cash flows. The criterion's underlying notion, that projects be chosen to retrieve capital outlays as quickly as possible, serves to reduce a firm's exposure to risk. Risk reduction as an objective, presumably, is not without merit. Still, a method such as payback that attempts to treat *both* the time phasing *and t*he uncertainty of future cash flows in an *ad hoc* manner—yet does neither very well—deserves little attention and even less praise in managerial economics today.

Equivalent Annual Cost

A popular capital budgeting concept in many applications, is that of equivalent annual total cost. It has been particularly favored by engineers evaluating alternative *designs* (of, say, a bridge or road) for performing much the same function (so that revenues or benefits can be asumed more or less identical, regardless of which design finally is adopted). Under such circumstances one need not worry about benefits or sales or revenues from the investment but can, instead, concentrate exclusively on finding the *lowest cost* solution or means of providing the specified stream of benefits, whatever they may be.

To compare total costs for projects involving both initial and annual cost components, it is necessary either to convert annual outlays into equivalent present values or to convert initial outlays into equivalent annual costs. Only when both components of cost are expressed in comparable units can they be combined to form a total cost figure which, in turn, can be used to describe and compare the costs associated with alternative ways of accomplishing the particular objective.

We already have seen in Eq. 4-1 how a stream of annual costs or returns can be discounted to form an equivalent present value; now let us see the opposite—how an initial (present) investment can be amortized uniformly over a number of time periods to form an equivalent *annual cost*. Equation 4-1 again provides our point of departure. Here, however, C will be used to denote an undertaking's initial cost; c will represent an equivalent series of equal, annual payments over $t = 1, 2, \ldots, n$ time periods, the project's economic life; r, as before, will measure the firm's or project's required return on capital; and equivalence is established if the following relationship is satisfied,

$$C = \frac{c}{(1+r)} + \frac{c}{(1+r)^2} + \cdots + \frac{c}{(1+r)^n}. \quad \text{(Eq. 4-2)}$$

As each period's annual cost is, by definition, exactly equal to any other's, c can be factored out of Eq. 4-2 and the relationship can be rewritten as

CAPITAL BUDGETING

$$C = c\left[\frac{1}{(1+r)} + \frac{1}{(1+r)^2} + \cdots + \frac{1}{(1+r)^n}\right]. \quad \text{(Eq. 4-3)}$$

After some mathematical manipulation, it also can be shown that Eqs. 4-2 and 4-3 are equivalent to the somewhat more complicated direct expression,

$$C = c\left[\frac{(1+r)^n - 1}{r(1+r)^n}\right]. \quad \text{(Eq. 4-4)}$$

All this may seem rather magical and unnecessary, and its purpose at this point may not be entirely clear. A very important point is emphasized by Eqs. 4-2, 4-3 and 4-4, however. It is that as one attempts to transform present costs and equivalent annual costs into one another, it is not enough simply to accumulate annual costs or amortize initial costs. One also must allow for differences in the times at which payments are made, by applying interest charges to outstanding balances. Only if returns on capital in alternative pursuits were zero, i.e., only if $r = 0$, would it follow from Eqs. 4-1, 4-2 and 4-3 that

$$C = c\,[1 + 1 \ldots + 1] = cn$$

or

$$c = \frac{C}{n}.$$

An example may help to illustrate. Suppose a physical asset were to cost $100 and were expected to last for five years. It is clear that a $100 current expenditure would not be *equivalent* in value to five annual $20 payments. No sensible person would pay $100 for the asset, then turn around and lease it to someone else on such terms. To account for differences in the time at which present and future cash payments are anticipated one could, if he wished, approximate interest charges on unpaid future obligations by multiplying the average value of annual capital charges by an appropriate interest factor. Thus, if charges on our $100 investment with a five-year life all were to come due on the last day of each year and, if the interest rate were 6 percent, one could say that interest costs during the first year would be approximately $.06 \times \$100 = \$6$; the second year, $.06 \times \$80 = \$4.80$, and so on. The problem would become slightly more complicated if returns were accrued continuously over the year; as for example, if the first year's interest cost were approximated by $.06 \times \$100 - \$80/2 = \$5.40$; the second year's by $.06 \times \$80 - \$60/2 = \$4.20$; and so forth.

To obtain the equal, annual payments that *exactly* amortize *both* interest *and* principal charges on any investment over its expected life, however, we could simply invert the right-hand-side of Eq. 4-4 and solve for annual costs c in terms of present costs C, as

$$c = C\left[\frac{r(1+r)^n}{(1+r)^n - 1}\right]. \qquad \text{(Eq. 4-5)}$$

Calculations such as these are encountered every day; by mortgage bankers converting an initial loan into equal monthly payments; by finance companies who purchase and lease computers, automobiles or other tangible assets to others; or by engineers, statisticians or economists who convert fixed outlays into annual charges for purposes of comparison, evaluation and, eventually, choice. When applied to capital budgeting evaluations, such charges are referred to as *capital recovery charges,* and the multipliers in brackets on the right-hand-side of Eq. 4-5 are referred to as *capital recovery factors*. The latter are tabulated for a wide range of capital costs, r, and economic lives, n, in standard texts on engineering economics, or as mortgage tables in banking texts, and in Table 3 of Appendix A.

When added to annual operating costs, capital recovery charges provide a perfectly defensible method of annualizing the total costs associated with any particular investment opportunity. As such, those total costs can provide a reasonably effective basis for evaluating and choosing between competing investment projects that do more or less the same thing (i.e., have the same benefits) yet have different economic lives. Should two or more investment opportunities have identical operating lives, a transformation of total costs from present value to annualized bases could not affect their *relative* rankings, as the capital recovery factor

$$\left[\frac{r(1+r)^n}{(1+r)^n - 1}\right]$$

that transforms present values into capital recovery charges would be the same for both. Thus, the project whose present value of total costs were the smallest also would carry the smallest equivalent, annual, total costs, and would do so by a constant fraction. An ability to perform such transformations still would be useful, as one must *either* collapse future operating expenses into a present value, *or* annualize initial costs through capital recovery charges to obtain total cost figures on either basis. The present method's clear advantage does emerge, however, as projects serving the same function but possessing different economic lives are encountered. Here the opportunity whose annualized total costs are smallest invariably provides the least cost alternative.

Again, an example may serve to illustrate. Suppose two milling machines capable of providing the *same* level of output per unit of time, and requiring the *same* operating inputs are considered for purchase. Assume the first costs $10,000 to buy and install, and is expected to last five years. Suppose the other costs $15,000 but is expected to last twice as long, a full ten years. If our company's cost of capital is around 8 percent, which is the better buy? That is, which machine can provide the indicated capacity per unit of time at the lowest cost per unit of time—or which offers the lowest cost per unit of capacity?

The present value of the first machine's capital costs, clearly, is lower than the second's (by exactly $15,000 − $10,000 = $5,000). As the second will last so much longer, however, comparisons on a straightforward present value basis may not be fully satisfactory. How can differences in durability be considered, systematically?

One way, clearly, would be to standardize for differences in economic lives by carrying comparisons to a common time horizon. Two successive five-year machines, for example, could be compared to a single ten-year machine on a present value basis. Or seven successive thirteen-year machines could be compared to thirteen successive seven-year machines over their lowest, common (91-year) time horizon. Conceptually such a procedure ought to be entirely satisfactory, and probably would provide good investment results. The fact that the procedure would be cumbersome computationally militates against its more general use, as does the violence done to practical men's sensibilities by assumptions of constant prices, technology and continual replacement over a 91-year (or even longer) time horizon.

Here, capital recovery, or equivalent annual cost methods provide a viable and attractive alternative, not because they lead to different decisions, but because they arrive at the same decisions from a more plausible set of starting assumptions—namely, that each investment is fully financed and paid off in uniform, annual installments covering both principal and interest payments over its own lifetime. The rate of interest charged, presumably, is not that which would be paid by the company were the machine actually financed through a bank but the rate of return obtainable by the company on other comparable investment projects. Using the 8 percent opportunity cost of capital hypothesized earlier, Eq. 4-5 permits us to calculate capital recovery factors of [.250] and [.149] for five- and ten-year investment lives (as in Table 3 of Appendix A), and through these, capital recovery charges for alternative pieces of milling equipment, of

$10,000 [.250] = $2,504 per year for five years, and

$15,000 [.149] = $2,235 per year for 10 years, respectively.

Which should be bought? Should one attempt to save $5,000 *now* by buying the initially lower cost machine, or to save $265 *per year* over ten consecutive years by buying the one that is cheaper on an annual basis, though more expensive to buy initially? Disregarding the uncertainty about the types of alternatives that will be available five years hence (when the first machine wears out), the more durable ten-year investment would appear to be the better buy.

Internal Rate of Return

One of the most commonly encountered discounting alternatives to present value, often advocated as a means of breaking the latter's dependence on the decision maker's specific choice of an interest rate, is called the *internal rate of return* criterion.[3] An internal rate of return may be defined as the rate of return (or the rate of interest) that equates the present value of an investment's returns with that of its capital outlays; or formally, as the rate r that satisfies the relation

$$C = V = \frac{y_1}{(1+r)} + \frac{y_2}{(1+r)^2} + \cdots + \frac{y_n}{1-r)^n} . \quad \text{(Eq. 4-6)}$$

where C, V and y are as defined earlier. Alternatively, an internal rate of return could be defined as the rate of time discount that reduces a project's net present value $V - C$ to zero.

Once again, an example may help to illustrate both the method's mechanics and some of its properties. Suppose an investor considers a project that, like all good textbook examples, costs $100 to obtain and set in operation. Suppose also that this undertaking promises to return $30 per year in addition to operating expenses over its five-year lifetime.

One way of evaluating such an opportunity's profitability would be to select an appropriate rate of interest and calculate the project's net present value, $V - C$. Suppose, however, that our investor really does not know what an appropriate rate of return for such a project would be. By turning to a present value table, however, he could determine that *if* $r = 4$ percent were the appropriate rate, the project's present value would be $34 greater than its cost. By repeating the process for other possible rates of return and plotting the resulting net present value-rate of discount couplets as in Fig. 4-4, our investor might quickly observe that any increase in his assumed rate of discount (by increasing the denominator of each term on the right-hand side of Eq. 4-2) reduces the present value of future returns to a *net present value of* $V - C = \$20$ for an 8 percent cost of capital, and an excess of present value over cost, $V - C = \$8$ for a 12 percent rate of return, and so on, until, at an interest rate of 15 percent, the project's net present value is wiped out entirely. Fifteen percent, then, is the rate of interest that equates the present value of the project's returns with its costs and is, accordingly, its internal rate of return. At even higher discount rates, of course, the venture's *net* present value becomes negative.

Properly and very carefully used, the internal rate of return may be made to yield essentially the same capital budget as present net value. However, proper use of internal rate of return is not always easy. When the capital budget is limited, so that not all projects with a net present value

---

[3] J. Dean, "Measuring the Productivity of Capital," *Harvard Business Review* (January-February 1954), reprinted in E. Solomon, ed., *op. cit.*

CAPITAL BUDGETING

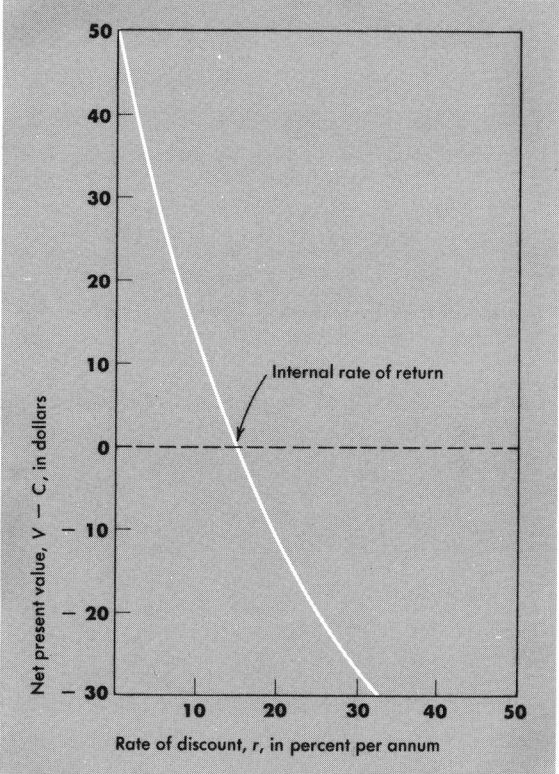

FIG. 4-4

greater than zero can be accepted, proper use of an internal rate of return criterion for project selection requires the making of incremental paired comparisons for each of the various possible project combinations. By contrast, present values are fairly easy to compute, even if one does not have access to a computer. To determine internal rates of return, on the other hand, it is necessary either to construct charts such as Fig. 4-4 for each investment alternative, or using an electronic computer, to solve Eq. 4-6 (which you will note, is a polynomial of degree n) directly for its root, r. Unfortunately, n degree polynomials may have more than one real solution; or in some instances may even have no meaningful solution.

These are purely mechanical, mathematical problems, however, that seldom are troublesome in actual applications. A more serious problem to potential decision makers might be the internal rate of return criterion's implicit assumption that the appropriate discount rate, r, for net benefits in each future year is the same as during any other year. Calculations of net present value, by contrast, can be considerably more flexible, in that one can readily employ different interest rates for different years if he so desires (that is, if a decision maker has some reason for believing that opportunity costs or yields on alternative uses of capital may be different during different future years).

Ranking and selecting projects according to an internal rate of return criterion also can lead to more incorrect selections of projects than a present value calculation, when not all projects are mutually exclusive, or when there is an absolute shortage of investment funds. These problems will be analyzed further in the next section.

In general, net present value will yield correct answers in every case where the internal rate of return criterion will do so and, furthermore, will do so in some instances where an internal rate of return criterion is very difficult to apply or breaks down altogether. Since net present values also are easier to calculate, are more flexible, and are not ambiguous in a mathematical sense, they generally are preferred to internal rates of return as a basis for project evaluation. Our basic rule for capital budgeting decisions, therefore, remains: *undertake an investment if the present value of future returns is greater than the asset's required capital outlay.*

SOME COMPLICATIONS: MULTIPLE PERIOD PLANNING AND BUDGET CONSTRAINTS

The theory of capital budgeting as outlined above has been developed almost entirely in the context of capital expenditures that are undertaken and completed during a single period of time. Actually, large projects often take several years to construct and may incur continuing losses for some period of time following the completion of construction. The fact that such projects can create net drains on a firm's capital resources over several consecutive years should be considered in a rational decision process.

The nature of this (multiple period planning) problem can be illustrated by a now classic example posed originally by Lorie and Savage.[4] They considered a situation in which there were nine alternative investment projects. Each involved capital outlays or costs during both of *two* years. All nine of the projects have positive net present values, but all nine cannot be undertaken simultaneously because of budget limitation on the amounts that can be expended during *each* of the two years. These budget limitations, or *constraints*, are $50 for the first year and $20 for the second year. The net present values and schedules of costs for years 1 and 2 are shown in Table 4-1 for all nine projects. As can be seen by inspecting costs in the table's two right-hand columns, it is quite clear that some of these projects

---

[4] J. Lorie and L. Savage, "Three Problems in Capital Rationing," *Journal of Business* (October 1955), reprinted in E. Solomon, ed., *op. cit.*

Table 4-1 THE LORIE-SAVAGE
MULTIPLE PERIOD BUDGETING

(1) Project Number	(2) Net Present Value, V_i	(3) Year 1 Costs C_{i1}	(4) Year 2 Costs C_{i2}
	($)	($)	($)
1	14	12	3
2	17	54	7
3	17	6	6
4	15	6	2
5	40	30	35
6	12	6	6
7	14	48	4
8	10	36	3
9	12	18	3
The budget constraint for:		Year 1 = $50	
		Year 2 = $20	

Source: Lorie and Savage, *Journal of Business* (October 1955); reprinted in E. Solomon, ed., *The Management of Corporate Capital*.

must be forgone if the firm is to stay within the constraints imposed by the two budget limitations on its capital expenditure program.

On the basis of the usual simple calculations of net present value, one might begin by concentrating on projects 2, 3, 4, and 5. However, it also is quite clear that project 2 exceeds the budget constraint of $50 for year 1 since its costs alone are $54 during that year. Excluding project 2 on these grounds, one might next concentrate on the combinations of 1, 3, 4, 5 and 3, 4, 5, 7 which seem second best in terms of cumulative net present value to the 2, 3, 4, 5 combination. But the 1, 3, 4, 5 and 3, 4, 5, 7 combinations also exceed the first year budget constraint of $50. By arranging projects in the order of their net present values per dollar of cost during the first time period (or by the ratio of elements in column 2 to those in column 3 for each project), the best combination of projects obtainable without violating the first year's budget constraint would be to select projects 3, 4, 6 and 5 in that order, having a cumulative first-year cost of $48 (and, therefore, remaining within the first year's $50 budget constraint). Specifically, this combination would provide the highest sum of net present values for any set of projects obtainable within the first year's capital budget.

The difficulty with this particular solution, however, is that the set 3, 4, 5, 6 creates second-year capital requirements of $49 that exceeds that year's $20 budget constraint by more than 2 to 1. Thus, *by looking only at the first period's capital budget, one would overcommit funds by 245 percent during the subsequent year.*

Lorie and Savage's proposal for solving this type of problem is of both historical and pedagogical interest. They proposed constructing a profitability index defined as

$$Z_i = V_i\, P_1 C_{i1} - P_2 C_{i2}$$

where Z_i defines a profitability index for the ith project,
V_i is the ith project's net present value,
P_1 is an imputed, or shadow price, for costs incurred during period 1,
P_2 is a similarly defined shadow price for costs incurred during period 2, and
C_{i1} and C_{i2} are costs for the ith project during periods 1 and 2, respectively.

Projects are to be selected in descending order of the profitability index, Z_i, which, it should be noted, is really a "corrected" net present value, reflecting the estimate of *opportunity costs* associated with outlays during different periods of time.

The solution procedure is fairly simple. To begin, one must choose a set of shadow prices P_1 and P_2 quite arbitrarily. All projects whose index Z_i is negative would be rejected. Projects having positive indices would constitute a trial solution for the problem.

The next step is simply to check and see whether or not every time period's budget constraints have been met. If, on inspection, it turns out that any one of these constraints, say for the second period as in the preceding example, has been exceeded, then the true costs of expending a dollar from that year's relatively more scarce capital resources have been underestimated, and the price, P_2 for that period should be increased to reflect this greater scarcity. On the other hand, should one period's budget be underspent on the first trial, our estimate of opportunity costs for expenditures from that period's budget ($P_1 C_{i1}$) would appear to be excessive and that period's assumed price (P_1) should be adjusted downward. The procedure, is repeated with new prices until an appropriate solution satisfying *all* the firm's budgetary limitations is obtained.

Clearly, the method has strong intuitive content. The profitability index and its shadow prices provide a method by which each project's interrelationship with the others, through their joint demands on the firm's scarce capital resources, is taken into account. The problem is to determine the *correct* shadow price to be attached to each year's capital expenditures.

The Lorie and Savage procedure generally will give a good approximation to the correct answer. However, it is basically a trial and error procedure (whose steps, unfortunately, are only vaguely defined) and can be a bit burdensome computationally. Furthermore, in a strict mathematical sense, there is no guarantee at all that a solution even exists or that once obtained, it is in fact optimal. Fortunately, there are some fairly simple mathematical programming techniques that can be used to solve the same class of problems in a more orderly and systematic fashion.[5] These techniques were discussed

---

[5] H. M. Weingartner, *Mathematical Programming and the Analysis of Capital Budgeting Problems* (Englewood Cliffs, N.J.: Prentice-Hall, Inc., 1963).

in Chapter Three. It should be noted in passing, however, that even mathematical programming techniques can yield misleading answers unless handled with care. In such applications it is well to have expert advice. At any rate, if one were to proceed with either the Lorie and Savage solution, or were to employ more sophisticated programming techniques to solve the problem, as outlined in Table 4-1, one would find that the set of projects maximizing attainable net present values while staying within the specified budget constraints would consist of projects 1, 3, 4, 6 and 9.

The important point to emphasize here, however, is not that multiple period planning problems can be handled in a systematic way but that their neglect can be dangerous. When constraints exist for *future* as well as for *current* budgetary periods, skillful optimization over the current period can provide only a correct answer to an incorrectly specified problem.[6] Should such myopia produce capital expenditure programs that exceed by a wide margin the firm's future capital resources, it may be extremely costly to the firm, its owners, and especially its management.

SOURCES AND USERS OF FUNDS AND THE COST OF CAPITAL

The calculation of net present value, even in simplest form, obviously has one indispensable requirement: someone must stipulate what value or values of the interest rate, r, are to be used for discounting purposes. This, in turn, raises a fundamental question regarding just what the cost of capital incurred by the firm in making such an investment may be, since almost by any definition, the discount rate, r, must bear some relationship to the firm's costs of raising funds, or of diverting funds from other uses to a particular expenditure.

Everything that has gone before in this book, and everything that will follow, suggests that this return must be based (at least conceptually) on an opportunity cost, and furthermore, that the opportunity cost in question

---

[6] Interdependence between project benefits and costs, other than through a budget, presents still another set of problems whose solutions are far from trivial. Interdependence would be a situation in which payoffs or costs of two different projects are affected by the other project's acceptance or rejection. Interdependent, *continuously variable projects* (that is, projects that do not have to be accepted in their entirety or otherwise rejected) can be treated in a reasonably straightforward fashion through the calculus of variations. Even if projects are discrete, that is, must be either accepted or rejected in their entirety, as well as being interdependent, the problem can be solved. When one has both interdependence and discreteness simultaneously, however, the problem's size can be expanded enormously. See for example, H. M. Weingartner, "On the Capital Budgeting of Interrelated Projects, Survey and Synthesis," *Management Science* (March 1966); and M. M. Hufschmidt, "Simulating the Behavior of a Multi-Unit, Multi-Purpose Water Resource System," in A. Hoggatt and F. Balderstone, eds., *Symposium on Simulation Models: Methodology and Applications to the Behavioral Sciences* (Cincinnati: South-Western Publishing Co., 1963).

must be that borne by the firm's owners in foregoing alternative uses for the funds. Beyond this initial presumption, however, it is easy to become mired in a mass of extremely messy details; for shareholders, clearly, have access to a variety of investment vehicles, each of which offers different risk and return combinations. *Which* alternative vehicle, and *which* rate of return should be used to capitalize any particular investment opportunity's expected cash flows often is a source of contention, both among managers and managerial economists.

Historically, economists have sought an answer to this question by focusing attention on returns available to the firm's owners through the purchase of proportionally larger fractions of all the company's outstanding securities, both debt and equity. By doing so, shareholders may effectively hold—and obtain investment returns on—a proportional share, not simply of the firm's equity, but of *all* its assets. Should the new capital budgeting project be comparable in all important respects to the types of assets already held, the rate of return at which existing cash flows are capitalized also should serve to *value* expected cash flows from the new undertaking.

There are several virtues to selecting a financial asset, or combination of financial assets, having the firm's risk characteristics as a basis for evaluating the company's cost of capital. First of all, a company can, in fact, usually sell these securities in open capital markets to provide a *source of funds* for direct investment purposes. Alternatively, the firm's own securities also may provide a perfectly satisfactory *use of funds* either for reinvestment by stockholders of dividend payments, or through the firm itself by repurchasing (and retiring) its own outstanding debt and equity securities. Both conceptually and practically, then, a firm's own securities may represent a very

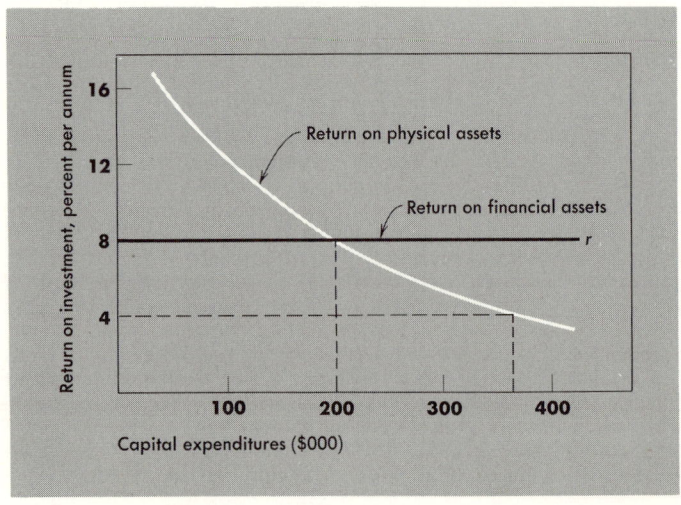

FIG. 4-5 A comparison of returns on physical and financial assets.

real investment opportunity that can either be purchased, if internally generated funds exceed the amounts needed for "real" investment opportunities, or can be sold to provide additional funds should the reverse be true. Consider, for example, the hypothetical, downward sloping demand curve for physical assets—"real investment" opportunities—in Fig. 4-5. Suppose in addition that returns on the company's securities are capitalized by investors in the securities markets at the $r = 8$ percent rate of return indicated by the figure's horizontal, straight line demand curve for financial assets. Rational investment policy for this (hypothetical) firm in an environment without taxes or transactions costs of any kind, then, would require the expenditure of precisely $200,000 on capital equipment; accepting *all* those projects whose rates of return exceed 8 percent, and *no* projects whose returns are less than that amount. Should internally generated funds fall short of the optimal $200,000 capital budget, additional shares could (and presumably should) be sold to raise the needed funds; should internally generated funds exceed $200,000, the remainder could be paid out as dividends to shareholders who, on their own, can obtain such returns (if they so desire) by purchasing additional securities on the open market.

The world in which most of us live, however, is not tax-free and also may contain non-negligible transactions costs for the purchase or sale of securities. Thus, corporate decisions to pay dividends, retain funds for investment in physical assets, raise additional capital through the sale of new securities, or use funds for the repurchase and retirement of outstanding securities may have a very important impact on each shareholder's well being. As a very simple example, consider a shareholder in the hypothetical corporation whose investment opportunities are displayed in Fig. 4-5 and whose marginal personal tax bracket is 50 percent. A dollar's worth of dividend payments to this investor, then, will add only 50 cent to his disposable personal income. Reinvested in additional shares of the firm's stock, this (before tax) dollar adds no more to its owner's welfare than would an investment by the firm itself in assets yielding as little as 4 percent. Thus, a perfectly rational management bent on maximizing its shareholder's welfare might well, in some circumstances, choose to retain earnings for investment in projects whose yields actually are less than the company's cost of capital.[7]

Internally generated funds, then, often are considered by managements to be low in cost. Saying the same thing differently, the *opportunity cost* of ploughing earnings back into a firm rather than distributing them as dividends to stockholders generally is not thought to be great. While such a view may be defensible from a managerial standpoint, it at least raises a question regarding whether or not stockholders value dividends differently from capital gains—that is, the increase in share price on the securities markets

---

[7] Theoretically, no corporation whose securities are publicly traded ever should encounter such a situation, for by repurchasing these securities the corporation can at least recover its capital costs—in our illustrative example, the 8 percent return on its own financial assets.

resulting from an increase in the firm's assets (generally from reinvested earnings) and earning power. If stockholders do not value dividends and capital gains differently, the sharp distinctions conventionally made between the costs of internal funds, long-term debt, preferred stock, and new stock issues are rather difficult to reconcile with the maximization of returns to ownership as a basic managerial objective.[8]

As a practical matter, of course, there usually are good reasons for stockholders to value dividends and capital gains quite differently. As already mentioned, for example, income from dividends and capital gains are taxed quite differently in the United States. Specifically, the maximum rate of taxation on capital gains normally is 25 percent, while that on dividends can be as high as 75 percent for persons in very high tax brackets. Furthermore, even if capital gains and dividends were taxed at identical rates, capital gains still might be somewhat preferred by a great many taxpayers, for the taxpayer himself has greater flexibility in choosing *when* he will be taxed; he can decide *when* he will sell his shares and, thereby, *realize* any taxable *gains*. Dividends, on the other hand, usually are taxed as they are received, leaving the average stockholder little choice over the timing of his tax liabilities. Being able to choose when to pay a tax gives the taxpayer an opportunity to delay the payment; this essentially provides him with an interest free loan from the government. As Section I of this chapter attempts to make clear, such a loan generally will be of considerable value to an astute investor.

The question of the cost of capital also can become intermingled with the measurement of risk. Quite obviously, if a firm can borrow unlimited sums of money at, say, 6 percent, it should do so—unless risk is a factor—as long as it has investment opportunities offering higher returns. Borrowing in this fashion is called *leveraging* the stockholders' investment. However, the extent to which various forms of fund raising are used, normally affects the firm's exposure to risk, imposing definite limits on the extent to which leverage or borrowing can be indulged. Conventional wisdom tells us that additional debt financing, other things being equal, will increase a firm's risk. Thus, lenders tend to insist at some point that additional debt be balanced by additional equity, either from the retention and reinvestment of internally generated funds or from the sale of additional shares of stock. Of course, if the proportions of debt to equity in the firm's capital structure were rigidly fixed, the relevant discount rate would simply be a weighted average of returns on the company's debt and equity securities. The difficulty

---

[8] See the following three articles by F. Modigliani and M. Miller: "The Cost of Capital, Corporation Finance, and the Theory of Investment," *American Economic Review,* 48 (1958); "Dividend Policy, Growth and the Valuation of Shares," *Journal of Business,* 34 (1961); and "Corporate Income Taxes and the Cost of Capital: A Correction," *American Economic Review,* 53 (1963). See also J. Linter, "The Valuation of Risk Assets and the Selection of Risky Investments in Stock Portfolios and Capital Budgets," *Review of Economics and Statistics* (February 1965).

with such an approach, obviously, is that risk appraisal generally is influenced importantly by the mix of debt and equity—and this, in turn, usually influences the *true costs* assigned both to borrowing and to the capitalization of the firm's equity securities.

Inflation or inflationary expectations also can condition the costs to a firm of borrowing. The rate charged for debt financing tends to increase as or if inflationary expectations arise. Debt generally represents a fixed obligation on the part of the borrower to pay a certain sum of money to the lender on a specified date. If general price inflation is expected, any fixed payment will be expected to decline in real purchasing power before repayment. In such circumstances, the lender often insists on a higher interest charge to offset his expected loss in real value. The cost of debt to a borrower depends, of course, on the extent to which the additional interest charge eventually offsets, or fails to offset, any subsequent decline in the purchasing power of money.

It also should be observed that under current stock market conditions many firms enjoy the enviable status of being thought to be so-called *growth* stocks. Generally speaking, a growth stock is an asset whose holders do not expect or even desire a large current dividend payment, but do expect considerable growth in the value of their holdings; that is, they expect to enjoy most of the return on their investment as capital gains. For firms that enjoy such status, new common stock issue may appear to be a relatively inexpensive means of financing certain kinds of capital acquisitions, especially the acquisition of other firms (through merger), as popularized by so-called conglomerate corporations.

In sum, the *cost of capital* as perceived by a firm's management can depend on a very large number of considerations: the structure of corporate and individual income taxes, the growth characteristics and reputation of the firm, the status of money markets (and, therefore, the interest rates charged on different classes of debt), the general state of the stock market and stockholders' expectations, and so forth. Under the circumstances, it is hardly surprising that most firms adopt a more or less arbitrary rule of thumb about the cost they will attach to their use of capital, and employ it as a discount rate in present value calculations. Typically, these rule of thumb estimates run between 8 and 20 percent (after taxes) for United States corporations, with exceptions usually lying above the higher rather than below the lower figure. Exact figures for any firm, or even for any particular capital budgeting decision, usually will be difficult to define with precision and will depend, for the reasons outlined, on the circumstances faced by the firm, its management and its stockholders. In a sense, this rule of thumb figure represents a distillation of managerial experiences regarding the costs of acquiring and using capital. The firm's management, by using such a figure, presumes that it can raise enough capital to meet all demands yielding such a return, and that by accepting all investments having such a yield, it will maximize the value to the firm's owners of the assets under their control.

Uncertainty

CHAPTER FIVE

THE NEED FOR ANALYSIS OF UNCERTAINTY

In development of the capital budgeting problem in the last chapter, our primary concern was the time phasing of net cash flows. Specifically, we focused on developing *criteria* through which the profitability of future cash flows for a particular investment opportunity can be summarized by a single, intuitively meaningful number (net present value) and by which different investment opportunities can be compared, and ranked. Net present value handles the time dimension of a large variety of capital budgeting problems effectively, *if an investment's future consequences can be foreseen with certainty.*

The future, of course, never can be foreseen with absolute certainty. Benjamin Franklin was right, as usual, when he observed that ". . . in this world, nothing is certain except death and taxes." Of what value, then, is present value, or any other criterion that assumes the future consequences of presents acts to be perfectly foreseeable? In the absence of a structure through which reasonable men can deal with uncertainty, of course, the answer must be that they are of limited value. To the extent that time and uncertainty are, or can be viewed, as separable elements of larger, overall decision problems, however, it may not be necessary to ignore one problem in order to treat the other; or worse, to turn to a criterion such as payback that treats both badly. A major thesis of this chapter is that uncertainty is such a separable problem, and that its treatment may be quite consistent with the use of a relatively precise criterion, such as net present value, for treating differences in the time profiles of alternative investment opportunities.

AN ILLUSTRATIVE EXAMPLE: WILDCATTING FOR OIL

Consider the following, illustrative problem [1] faced by Mr. Norman L. Jones, the president and major shareholder of a relatively small domestic oil producer, whose sales currently are running at about $10 million per year, yielding after-tax earnings of approximately $1-½ million per year, and whose annual exploration expenditures vary between $2 and $3 million. The company has an option to explore for oil and gas on forty acres of West Texas land. If not exercised within the next four weeks, the option will expire; so Jones must come to a decision without further delay.

Since obtaining this option nearly four years ago, extensive exploratory drilling by other operators has confirmed the existence and apparent boundaries of a sizeable field of oil and natural gas pools in the area surrounding the company's site. Although the site, clearly, is in the field's productive zone, any particular well's productivity is determined largely by subsurface geological formations and, therefore, is difficult to predict. Since exploration of the field began, 70 wildcat wells have been completed, 21 of which are dry (nonproductive), 28 are gas wells, 14 combination oil and gas pools, and 7 are oil wells.

The after-tax cost of drilling a well on this site would be about $100,000. From trade association data, as well as his own experience in the area, Mr. Jones is able to determine with a high degree of accuracy the average amount of oil and gas reserves recoverable from a successful well in the field. Considering the company's (14 percent) after-tax cost of capital, a typical gas well should yield a net present value of $150,000, a combination well $200,000, and an oil well $300,000; these figures would be after taxes, capital costs, royalty payments and operating expenses, but before the estimated $100,000 cost of drilling, which can be considered the project's capital outlay.

Several major oil companies in the area have employed an exploration technique untried by Mr. Jones' company, called a *seismic test* to determine the type of subsurface formation below a proposed drilling site. The test

---

[1] Similar situations are described in C. Jackson Grayson's *Decisions Under Uncertainty: Drilling Decisions by Oil and Gas Operators,* Harvard Business School, Division of Sponsored Research, 1960; Gordon M. Kaufman's *Statistical Decision and Related Techniques in Oil and Gas Exploration* (Englewood Cliffs, N.J.: Prentice-Hall, Inc., 1963); John W. Pratt, Howard Raiffa and Robert Schlaifer's *Introduction to Statistical Decision Theory,* Preliminary Edition (New York: McGraw-Hill Book Company, 1965); and in a variety of Harvard Business School Cases, including Neil Harlan, Richard Vancil and Gordon Kaufman's "The Waco Wildcat Company," Case 4C43R, available through the Intercollegiate Case Clearing House, Harvard Business School, Boston, Massachusetts.

requires a highly trained crew to bury and detonate an explosive charge and expensive equipment to record the resulting shock waves. After interpreting the seismograph, geologists are able to predict subsurface formations with a high degree of accuracy.

Three main types of formations are commonly found in the area. Of the 30 seismic tests "shot" nearby, type "A" formations (generally thought to be unproductive) have been indicated 12 times; type "B" formations (likely to contain gas pools) 15 times; and type "C" formations (which almost always yield an oil well) 3 times.

Except for type "A" formations, which seldom are drilled, subsequent drilling has invariably confirmed the seismic test's predictions. Of the four "A" formations drilled, three were dry and the fourth yielded a gas well. Of the 15 type "B" formations drilled, nine were gas producers and the other six were combination oil and gas wells; while "C" formations, in each case, have yielded oil wells. The cost of running a seismic test, unfortunately, is $30,000.

Should the company decide neither to drill nor to test the site, it could sell the option for $15,000. Should a seismic test be run and yield negative results, however, no speculator would touch the site and the option would become worthless immediately.

Reviewing this information, President Jones feels that all the facts necessary to make his decision are at hand. As a first step in putting these facts together, however, he removes a yellow pad from his desk and begins to sketch a *decision tree* that eventually becomes Fig. 5-1. The tree, really, is nothing but a schematic representation of the manner in which this particular decision's consequences (monetary payoffs) are related to alternative possible *acts, strategies* or *decisions* open to the company (such as drill, test, or sell) and to uncertain possible *events* (such as the presence of oil, gas, both or neither on the site) that necessarily are beyond the company's control.

Reduced to bare essentials, as in Fig. 5-1, a decision tree may be nothing more than a convenient device for organizing and presenting essential elements of the factual information required for a managerial decision under uncertainty. In general, however, a decision tree is much more than simply a passive device for displaying information; it also is a potentially powerful tool for decomposing complex decision problems into less complex problems, whose solutions are both tractable and equivalent to the original problem faced by the decision maker.

Let us consider Jones' problem as it appears to him now, standing at the left-hand side, or *fork*, of Fig. 5-1's decision tree. His immediate task is, simply, to decide which of three initial actions to take, or branches to follow, from his present position. In evaluating the relative desirability of each present decision, however, Jones must keep in mind a large number of simultaneous considerations, including the relative desirability of several possible future consequences, most of which are not under his control, but

UNCERTAINTY

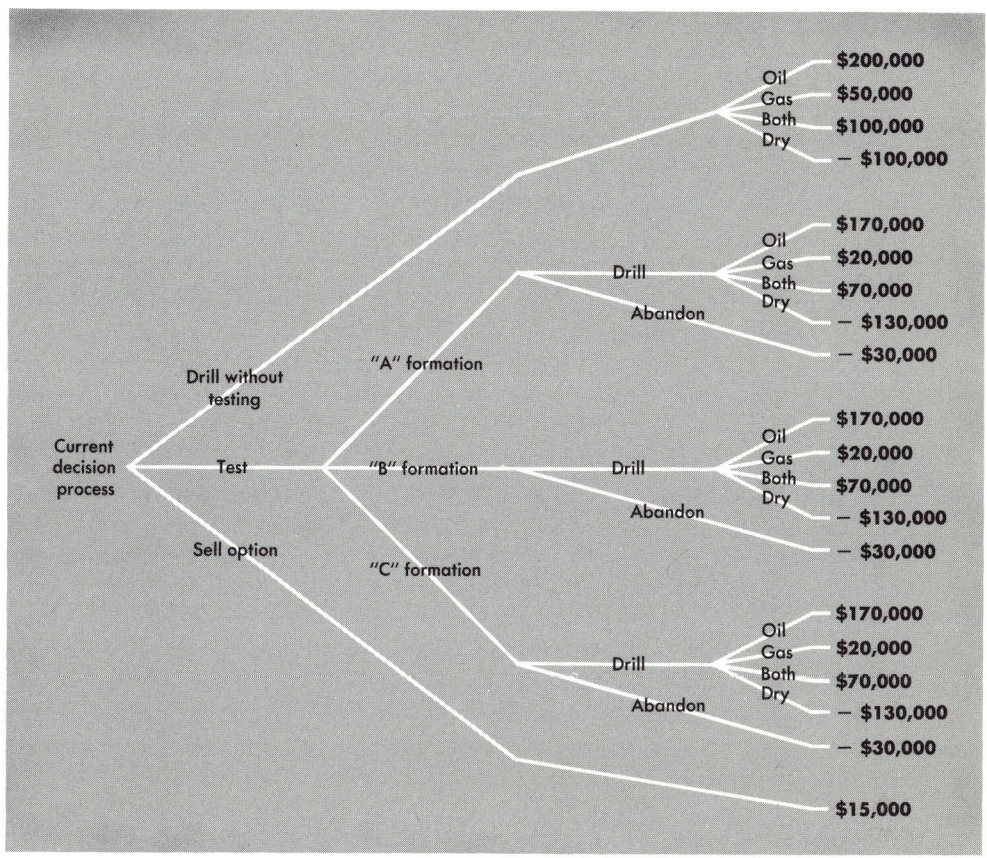

FIG. 5-1 Complete drilling decision tree.

some of which also depend at least partially on his own future acts, or drilling decisions.

Should Jones decide to take the lower branch of the decision tree by selling the company's option, he immediately arrives, of course, at the right-hand side of the diagram, or at a *terminal act*, whose monetary consequences (receive $15,000) are known with certainty and, accordingly, are easily evaluated.

Should Jones choose the upper branch, "Drill Without Testing," however, he must wait to see whether nature, or chance, will lead him along the branch (or to the terminal event) for "Oil Discovered," "Gas Discovered," "Both Oil and Gas Discovered," or "Dry Hole Discovered." Once his decision to drill (or not to drill) has been made, however, the terminal event leading to definite monetary consequences is no longer under his control. Should a drilling decision be followed by the discovery of oil, nature will reward the company with a $200,000 addition to its net present value, after all expenses (including the capital outlay of $100,000) have been deducted; should the discovery of gas follow a drilling decision, $50,000 will be the company's reward for risk taking; should a combination oil and gas pool be discovered, $100,000 will be gained; while a dry hole will cost the company every penny of its $100,000 drilling expense.

The tree's middle branch is even more difficult for Jones to evaluate directly; for here the array of possible monetary consequences that nature, eventually, will award the company are further conditioned by the set of future acts the company itself may take. Jones, therefore, must not only evaluate the desirability of three hypothetical future gambles (represented by three different drilling samples, or terminal event forks) but also must consider *now* what decision he would make *then* (regarding drill or abandon tract) should a seismic test indicate the presence of either type "A," "B," or "C" subsurface formations.

The simultaneous considerations of so many future gambles, some of which are conditional on additional future decisions, clearly, is far from trivial. Yet this is precisely what a decision maker like Jones must somehow balance if he is to attempt a direct solution of this (relatively simple) decision problem under uncertainty. One advantage of a decision tree, such as Fig. 5-1, is that it clarifies the nature of Jones' problem and the options that, in his opinion, are worth considering; another is that it organizes the important information required for the problem's solution; and a third, mentioned earlier, is that it decomposes his overall problem into a number of smaller and more tractable subproblems, none of which is trivial, but all of which are considerably less difficult to evaluate separately than together. Let us examine these smaller problems individually, to see how their separate evaluation may contribute to a viable solution for Jones' actual (overall) decision problem.

VALUATION BY CERTAINTY EQUIVALENCE

Returning to the third of Jones' options, sell immediately for $15,000, it is clear that no uncertainty and, therefore, no evaluation problem exists. Jones, presumably, will be happy to trade his access to this branch of the decision tree for any amount greater than $15,000 and will refuse to do so for any lesser amount. Or, to use a more esoteric term, Jones would be indifferent between this and any other *certain* payment of $15,000. In short, the *certain* receipt of $15,000 is worth exactly $15,000, neither more nor less.

To compare actions whose consequences are known with certainty to other actions whose possible outcomes are not certain, however, Jones must be able to reduce the latter (such as the topmost "terminal drilling gamble" in Fig. 5-1) to an *equivalent, certain* sum of money. Specifically, he must be able to answer hypothetical questions about the amount of money he would (just) be willing to accept in exchange for an opportunity to "Drill Without Testing"; or for the opportunity to undertake any other "terminal gamble."

Jones does in fact have *immediate* access to the "Drill Without Testing" gamble. It seems reasonable, therefore, for Jones to ask himself just what such an opportunity is worth? Presumably, it is worth less (or at least, not *more*) than the *most* favorable of its possible outcomes (strike oil, and receive $200,000). Presumably, also, the gamble is worth more (or at least, not *less*) than the *least* favorable, or most disastrous, of its outcomes (drill a dry hole, and lose $100,000). How much less than $200,000 or more than − $100,000 this gamble is worth *to Jones,* depends both on his judgments concerning the probability of actually obtaining each possible outcome and on his preferences for alternative outcomes given his current financial situation; or more explicitly, on his views concerning both the *probability* and the *importance* of actually obtaining any particular monetary payments from the gamble.

One could imagine, for example, that if Jones were virtually certain oil would be discovered on the site, he would be willing to accept very little less than $200,000 for the opportunity to drill. Similarly, were he virtually certain that a dry hole would result, he would prefer to abandon the site.

Jones must also balance his views about the probability of obtaining alternative outcomes against his preferences for these outcomes should they actually be obtained. Would a $100,000 "dead loss" turn out to be disastrous to the firm? Would Jones go under if two or three dry holes in a row were drilled? Or would a $200,000 profit stave off impending bankruptcy? Would it permit the company to turn an important corner in its corporate development?

Just how Jones is to balance his judgments concerning the relative probability of, and his preferences for, alternative outcomes from a gamble such as "Drill Without Testing" need not concern us at the moment. (We shall return to these questions in subsequent sections of the chapter.) What is of concern, however, is how Jones would *use* this information *if he had it* to simplify the decision problem diagrammed in Fig. 5-1.

Suppose that Jones, using intuition acquired from his years of experience as an oil wildcatter, is able to decide that his present opportunity to "Drill Without Testing" would be *worth* $20,000 to him, i.e., that he would be willing to pay up to $20,000 in exchange for the opportunity to drill on this site without further information, and would be willing to sell the opportunity for any greater amount. (For the moment, we shall not be concerned "how" Jones arrives at this intuitive judgment but only that he makes it; later in the chapter we shall discuss the "how.") The gamble

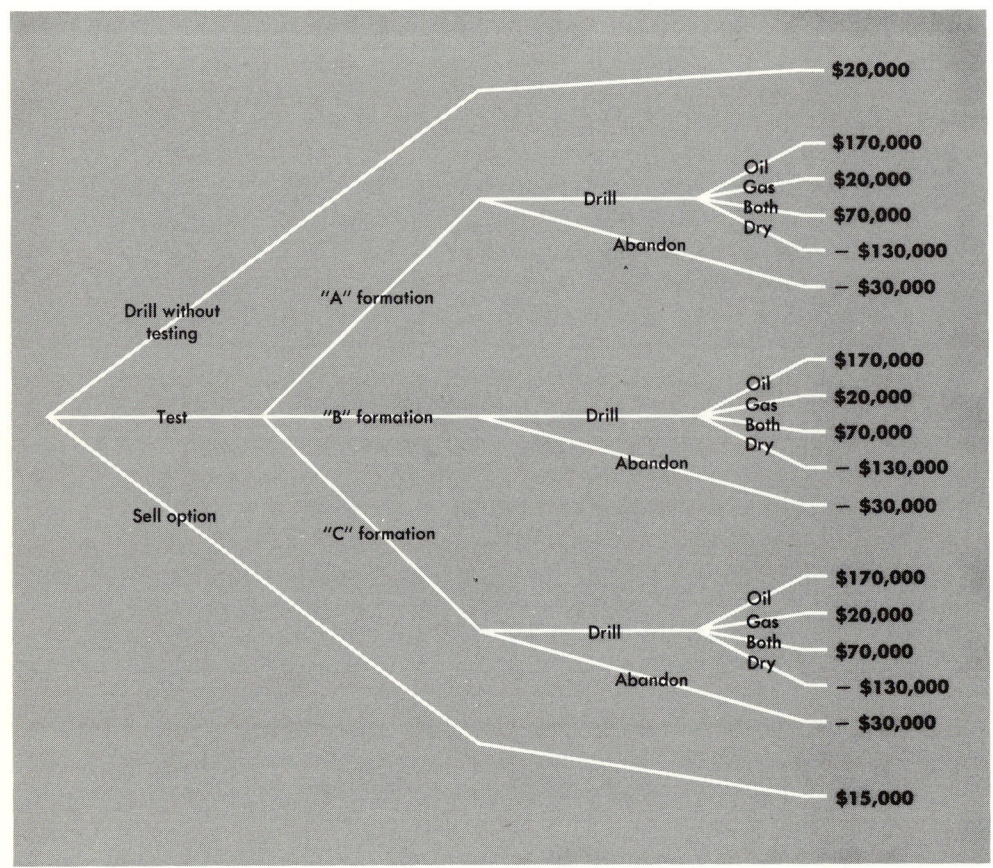

FIG. 5-2 Equivalent, simplified drilling decision tree.

whose uncertain monetary consequences are summarized in Fig. 5-1's topmost drilling fork, then should appear *equivalent* in Jones' mind to the *certain* receipt of exactly $20,000.

Jones' ability to make such a statement is extremely important—indeed, it is *essential* if he is to arrive at a sensible course of action or solution for his "decision problem under uncertainty." Schematically, Jones' ability to make such a judgment permits the topmost terminal event fork (or gamble) in Fig. 5-1 to be replaced by the *equivalent certain* terminal value, receive $20,000, shown as the topmost branch of Fig. 5-2. Thus, Fig. 5-1 can be replaced by the simpler *equivalent* decision diagram summarized in Fig. 5-2.

Were Jones' decision limited to two possible courses of action, "Drill Without Testing" or "Sell Option," his choice now would be clear. A rational man, presumably, would prefer $20,000 *for certain* to $15,000 *for certain*, and similarly, would prefer a gamble (Drill Without Testing) whose uncertain value is *equivalent* to the *certain* receipt of $20,000 to any other act (such as "Sell the Option") whose value is less. If not, Jones either is "kidding himself" when he asserts that the gamble (drill without testing) has a value *equivalent* to the *certain* receipt of $20,000, or his choice is not consistent with the relatively fundamental precept that "more generally is preferred to less."

Jones' decision is not limited, however, to two possible courses of action but includes a third, "Perform Seismic Test," whose consequences are conditioned both by two distinct stages of uncertainty, and by his own reaction to the first of these stages. To evaluate this composite act-event sequence it will be necessary for Jones to decide *now* what the value of each of his possible future *acts* (or decisions) would be should seismic testing reveal type "A," "B," or "C" subsurface formations.

Despite the fact that the act of performing a seismic test does not by itself change the overall probability foreseen *now* by Jones of striking oil, gas, both, or neither, the test's result certainly will affect the attractiveness to him of an opportunity to drill in this area. Should an "A" formation be located, for example, Jones may virtually rule out the possibility of finding oil on the site, either by itself or in combination with gas. Indeed, should experience serve as a reliable guide, the two alternative outcomes to be expected from a decision to "drill" on an "A" formation are likely to be, simply: gas is discovered, yielding a well worth $20,000 net of drilling and testing expenditures; or a dry hole is discovered, resulting in the total loss of $130,000. Jones may, as a result, simplify the terminal gamble corresponding to "Test, 'A' formation discovered" in Fig. 5-1 from the four-branch terminal event fork diagrammed there to the simplified two-branch terminal event fork diagrammed in Fig. 5-2, and on the left-hand side of Fig. 5-3.

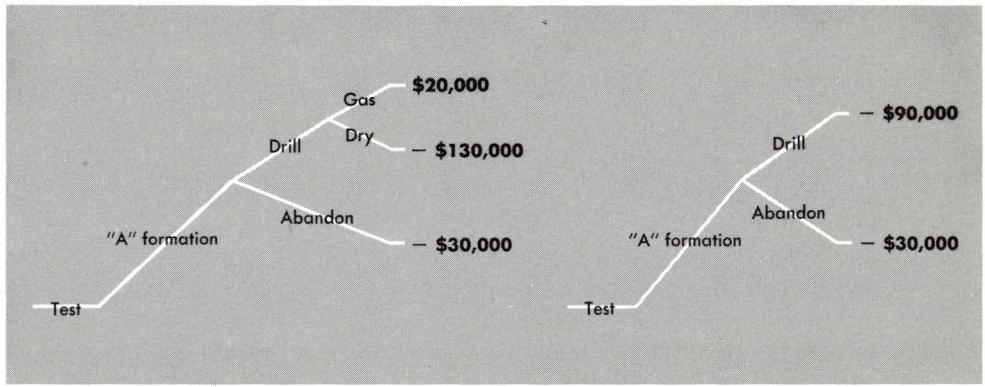

FIG. 5-3 Terminal decision: "A" formation.

Furthermore, the value to Jones of "drilling" on an "A" formation is likely to be heavily influenced by his knowledge that, in the past, an overwhelming preponderance of wells on such formations have turned out to be dry. The opportunity to drill on such a formation, then, probably is not considered preferable to the decidedly unattractive option of abandoning the site altogether and forfeiting for *certain* the $30,000 cost of conducting the seismic test. In fact, an opportunity to drill on so unfavorable a formation might be reduced by Jones to a *certainty equivalent* of, say, − $90,000; that is, he would just as soon lose $90,000 *for certain* as accept the rather small chance of gaining $20,000 (against the very large, complementary chance of losing $130,000) by drilling on an "A" formation.

By arriving at this evaluation, Jones has simplified that branch of his decision diagram corresponding to "Test, 'A' formation discovered," by substituting the *equivalent* terminal value of −$90,000 on the right-hand side of Fig. 5-3 for the corresponding terminal *gamble* on the figure's left-hand side. Once this has been done, of course, the next step is obvious. Jones will, figuratively, "chop off" the branch corresponding to "drill," by deciding that *if* a seismic test were to indicate an "A" formation, he would choose to *abandon* rather than *drill* the site. Schematically, then, Jones has simplified the entire branch of his decision diagram corresponding to "Test, 'A' formation discovered," from that summarized in Figs. 5-1 through 5-3 to the

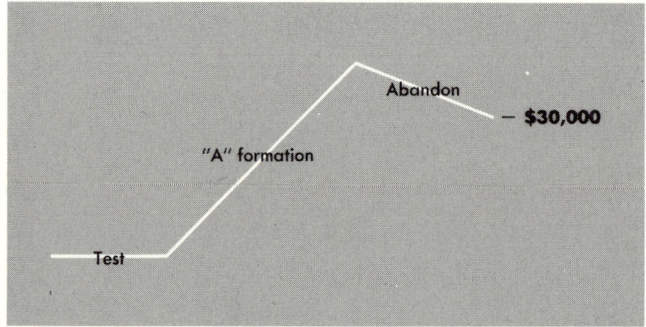

FIG. 5-4 Equivalent terminal value: "A" formation.

equivalent terminal value, or *certainty equivalent* reproduced in Fig. 5-4. By "rolling back" his decision tree in this fashion, Jones has, in fact, solved two separate and extremely important problems; he has decided *now* what he would do in the future *if* seismic testing should locate an "A" formation, and has determined the *value* to himself of this (rather melancholy) event.

Let us next assume that Jones can repeat this procedure for the middle branch of his "Test" alternative, i.e., for that portion of the overall decision tree corresponding to "Test, 'B' formation discovered." As before,

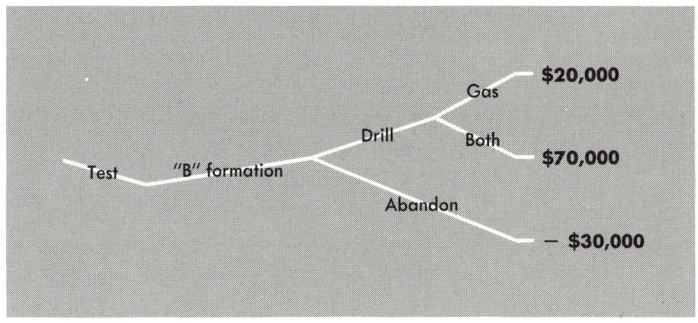

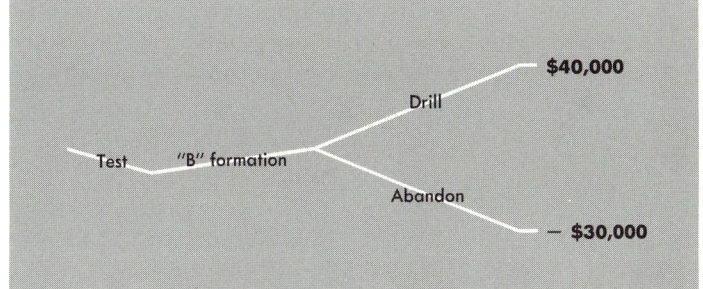

FIG. 5-5 Terminal decision: "B" formation.

the value to Jones of this (much more favorable) event depends ultimately on his assessment of the *value* to himself of the resulting terminal (drilling) gamble, and on his implicit future decision (regarding drill or abandon claim) that follows the assessment. As our decision maker is virtually certain that any well drilled on a "B" formation will lead to the discovery of gas, either by itself or in combination with oil, he is likely to simplify this portion of his decison tree by reducing it to the two branches or outcomes of either finding gas (worth $20,000) or a combination of gas and oil, (worth $70,000), diagrammed on the left-hand side of Fig. 5-5. In order to proceed with his evaluation, Jones next must ask himself "how much the opportunity to drill on a 'B' formation" in this area would be worth?

Again, let us assume that our decision maker, as a rational man, would consider the opportunity to be at least as valuable as the smallest of its foreseeable payoffs (discover gas, receive $20,000) but no more valuable than its most favorable outcome (discover a combination oil and gas pool, and receive $70,000). After pondering this question, again drawing on his experience and intuition, let's assume that Jones is able to decide that he would in fact trade the opportunity to drill on a "B" formation for exactly $40,000. Schematically, then, he has moved himself from the middle branch of his "Test" alternative in Fig. 5-1 to the simpler, equivalent diagram on the right-hand side of Fig. 5-5.

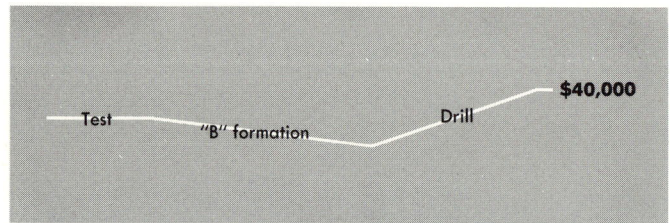

FIG. 5-6 Equivalent terminal value: "B" formation.

Jones' next step, of course, is as trivial as it is mechanical. By making this essential judgment on the equivalent certain value of locating this formation, he has effectively decided *now* both what he would do in the future *if* seismic testing should reveal a "B" formation, and what the *value* to him

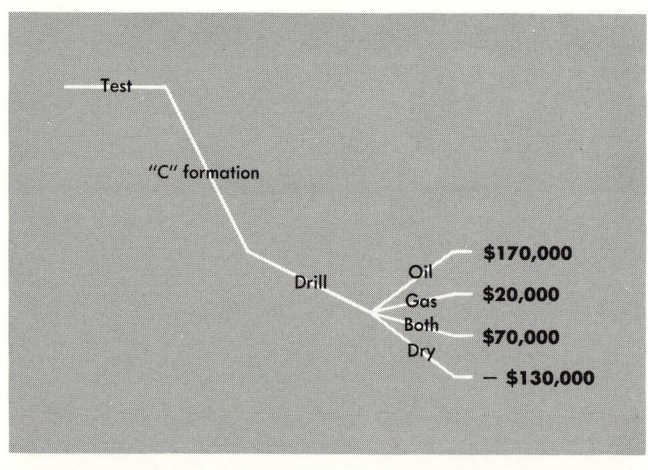

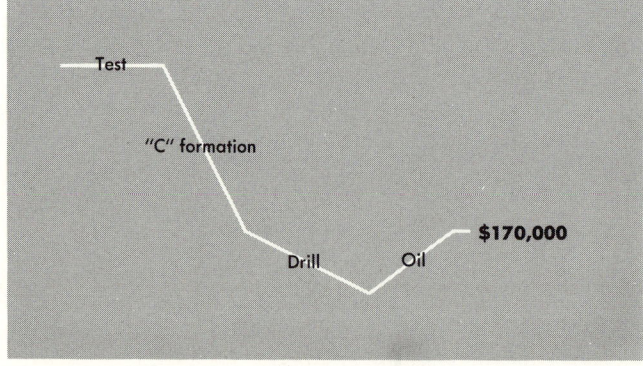

FIG. 5-7 Terminal drilling gamble: "C" formation.

of the discovery would be. He has, for all practical purposes "chopped off" the branch of Fig. 5-5's decision tree corresponding to "Abandon Site," by deciding that *if* a "B" formation were discovered he would *drill,* and schematically, has replaced Fig. 5-5's decision diagram by the single, equivalent $40,000 terminal value summarized in Fig. 5-6.

The third and final branch of Jones' "Test" alternative, that corresponding to "Test, 'C' formation discovered," can similarly be "rolled back" from the terminal gamble summarized in Fig. 5-1 and repeated on the left-hand side of Fig. 5-7, to the *certainty equivalent* diagrammed on its right-hand side. From experience, Jones knows that "C" formations virtually always yield an oil well, and that in this field all three previous seismic "C" findings have been followed by oil discoveries. Should he conclude, therefore, that a seismic "C" outcome is virtually tantamount to the location of oil, he may immediately eliminate all other possibilities and simplify his formal terminal event fork for "Test, 'C' formation discovered" from Fig. 5-7's left-hand gamble, to the single branched, *certain* outcome (discover oil, receive $170,000) on it's right-hand side.

By making this simplification Jones is, basically, asserting that *in his view* the location of a seismic "C" formation eliminates further uncertainty

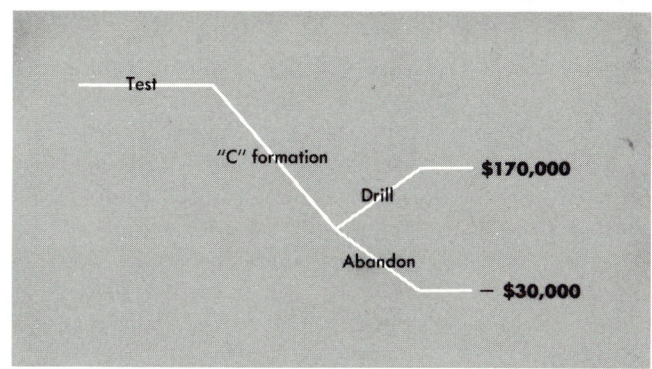

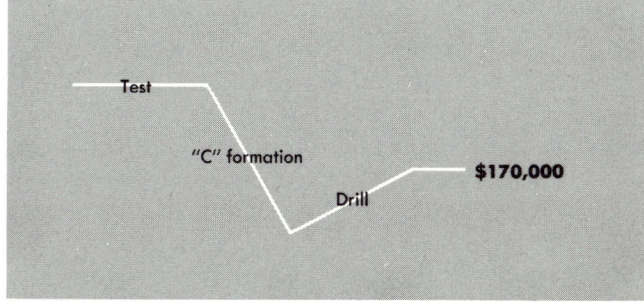

FIG. 5-8 Terminal decision, and equivalent terminal value: "C" formation.

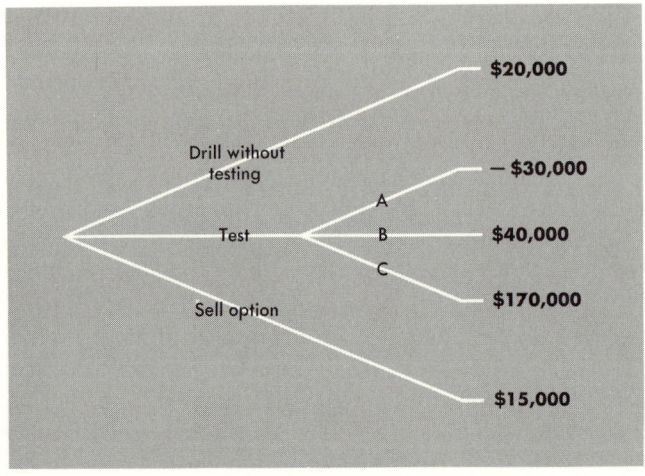

FIG. 5-9 Equivalent, simplified decision tree.

from this decision problem. Other persons, equally familiar with the degree of skill and care that go into seismic tests, may not agree; but Jones' decision is and must remain his own and, therefore, must be based on his assessment of the value to the firm of this or any other drilling opportunity. Should he, therefore, after due deliberation, decide that the opportunity to drill on a "C" formation is worth $170,000, no further information would be required either about his confidence in the test's validity or about his assessment of its value to the firm. His conditional, terminal drilling decision could be summarized simply by the two-branch decision fork on the left-hand side of Fig. 5-8. Without further ado, he clearly would erase (and perhaps even burn) the diagram's lower branch; for it is quite inconceivable that a dead loss of $30,000 from abandoning the site would be preferred to the opportunity worth $170,000 of drilling on a "C" formation.

By making this essential judgment, Jones has decided *now* both that *if* seismic testing should reveal a "C" formation, he will *drill,* and that the value to the firm of such a discovery would be *equivalent* to the *certain* receipt of $170,000.

In summary by going through these exercises, Jones has effectively decided *both* what he would do in the future *if* a seismic test should reveal either type "A," "B," or "C" subsurface formations, and what each of these discoveries would be worth. He has decided, for example, that *if* an "A" formation were discovered, he would abandon the site and accept the implicit, certain loss of $30,000. He also has decided that should either seismic "B" or "C" formations be discovered, he would drill, and that these opportunities would be equivalent in value to *certain* cash payments of $40,000 and $170,000 respectively. Jones has, then, effectively, equated a set of *uncertain terminal* gambles and implicit future courses of action to a corresponding set of *equivalent terminal values* and, in the process, has reduced his initial decision problem from the relatively complex "total decision" diagrammed in Fig. 5-1 to the much more simple yet entirely *equivalent* substitute problem diagrammed in Fig. 5-9.

If Jones has done his homework carefully and if, as a result, the terminal values on the right-hand side of Fig. 5-9's branches accurately reflect his assessment of the *value* to the firm of the act-event sequences they replace, then a solution for the original problem is close at hand. The only remaining problem is to evaluate the *simple gamble* summarized by the figure's remaining terminal event fork, "Test," and: if "A," receive—$30,000; if "B," receive $40,000, and if "C," receive $170,000. By balancing in his own mind the relative probabilities of obtaining alternative seismic results against the monetary consequences implicit in each result, let us assume that Jones is able to reduce this gamble, like any conventional drilling gamble, to a *certain, monetary equivalent*. Furthermore, assume that the attractiveness to Jones of reducing by $70,000 his maximum, foreseeable monetary loss (by "Abandoning site without drilling" should an "A" formation be discovered), against the relatively small $30,000 cost imposed by the test on more favorable outcomes, leads him after full deliberation to decide that an opportunity to conduct such a test would be worth $25,000 (net of costs) to the firm.

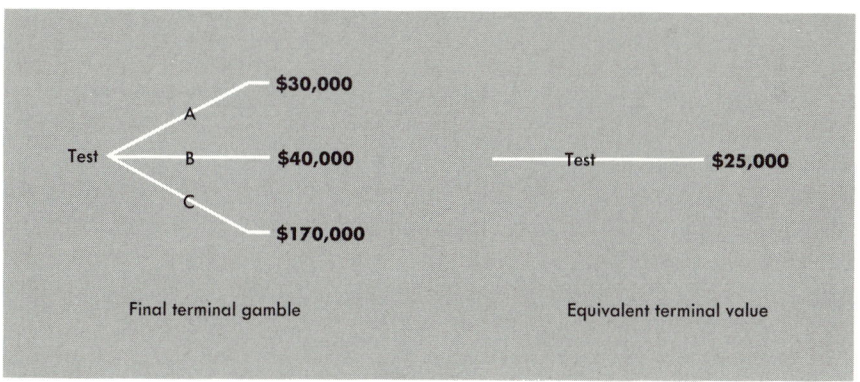

FIG. 5-10 Seismic "test" alternative.

Schematically, then, Jones has reduced Fig. 5-9's final terminal gamble from the event fork summarized there, or on the left-hand side of Fig. 5-10, to the equivalent *terminal value* on Fig. 5-10's right-hand side.

Jone's decision, then, has been made. By starting with each of Fig. 5-1's uncertain terminal gambles and reducing them in turn to equivalent terminal values—i.e., to certain cash payments that he would *just* be willing to accept *now* in exchange for each gamble if and when it should actually be faced—

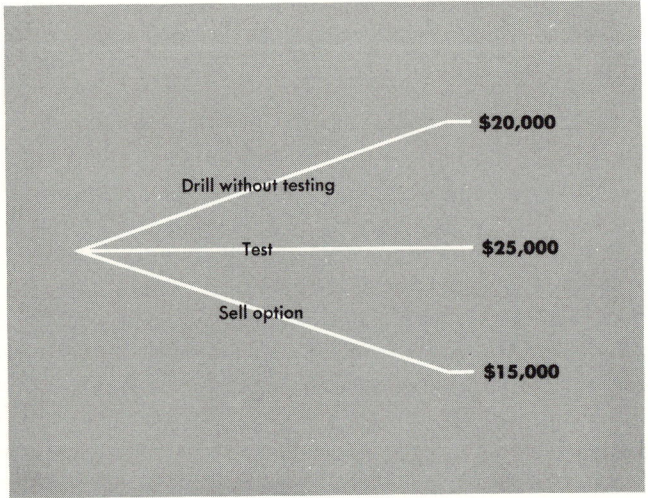

FIG. 5-11 Final, equivalent decision diagram following reduction to certainty equivalents.

Jones has, systematically, reduced each terminal *act* to a set of equivalent terminal *values,* whose greatest value, or branch, serves in turn as an end position for the uncertain gamble next down the line. The process is repeated, of course, until each *initial act* has been fully evaluated, or "rolled back" to the decision maker's current position at the tree's left-hand node. Once the tree's final terminal gamble has been reduced (as in Fig. 5-10) to a single, equivalent terminal value, the process is complete and Jones can arrive at a decision that is consistent both with his beliefs about the relative probability of obtaining alternative possible outcomes and his judgments concerning the relative desirability of obtaining them, from each of his problem's embedded gambles. Given Jones' beliefs and attitudes, developed and summarized in the process of "roll back" to the certainty equivalents summarized in Fig. 5-11, it is clear that his optimal initial act is to "Test"; followed by a somewhat more complex overall strategy that could be described as "Test and if 'A' formation is discovered abandon site; if 'B' or 'C' formations are discovered, drill."

VALUATION BY EXPECTED VALUES

Despite its seeming plausibility, there are any number of reasons why Jones may not be satisfied with the certainty equivalence solution just outlined. He may doubt that his initial decision tree accurately represents the structure of acts and gambles faced by the firm; or that net cash flows *fully* describe the value of attaining particular end positions. This type of dissatisfaction, however, is entirely specific to individual applications. If a decision tree does not adequately represent the decision maker's perception of his problem's structure, it should be modified until it does, and if net cash flows do not adequately summarize the value to the firm of attaining particular end positions, they should be adjusted until they do.[2]

Jones' most persistent and nagging doubts about the usefulness of the approach to decision making under uncertainty outlined above, however, are likely to center on his ability to evaluate large numbers of terminal gambles with a reasonable degree of logical *consistency*. Jones is aware, of course, that his solution to any decision problem involving uncertainty turns *crucially* on his choice of *certainty equivalents* for each and every gamble encountered (or created) as a decision tree is "rolled back" toward its source. He also is aware that his own unaided intuition is likely to be a somewhat imperfect tool for *consistently* balancing the relatively subtle and delicate mixture of probabilistic and subjective information (regarding the relative probability and importance of alternative possible payoffs) that necessarily underlies any gamble's *equivalent,* certain value. That is, he is likely to recognize that attempts on his part to *directly assess* the relative values of large numbers of separate gambles, in isolation, almost certainly will lead him into a considerable number of logical "traps."

Laboratory experiments have demonstrated that even the most highly trained of persons [3] are easily led into sets of direct assessments that contain either reversals in the relative desirability of "identical" pairs of gambles at different points in time;[4] or that lack transitivity at a given point in time; or that suffer from both types of short-comings simultaneously. Logical pitfalls of this sort are virtually inevitable if direct assessment alone is applied to numerous gambles on an item-by-item basis. Jones, certainly, will be distressed by the possibility of such entirely human "mistakes" in his own "directly assessed preferences."

To avoid such inconsistencies, it may be necessary for Jones to back off from a particular decision problem long enough to ask himself "how his assessments of the magnitude and probability of a gamble's alternative possible outcomes *should* be combined to form a certainty equivalent?" By his answer to this question Jones may be able to build greater consistency into his analysis of decisions under uncertainty by replacing fully intuitive item-by-item *assessments* with logically equivalent, objective *calculations*. Such a calculation, of course, must simultaneously reproduce Jones' preferences for

---

[2] For further discussion of these and related problems, see Robert Schlaifer's, *Analysis of Decisions Under Uncertainty,* (New York: McGraw-Hill Book Company, 1967).

[3] Including Leonard J. Savage, a pioneer in the development of statistical decision theory; see the amusing description of Savage's embarrassment, in Robert D. Luce and Howard Raiffa's, *Games and Decisions* (New York: John Wiley & Sons, Inc., 1958), Chapter 2.

[4] During which no information arose to change either the character of the gambles themselves, or the decision maker's situation and attitude toward risk.

alternative gambles on an item-by-item basis without violating his preferences (by being logically inconsistent) over a broader spectrum of choice. In short, Jones seeks a *procedure* for *evaluating* risky ventures that is consistent with his preferences toward risk, both in the large and the small.

One such procedure, that characterizes a broad range of business choices under uncertainty, is called *expected value*. Although the preference structure regarding risk that underlies it is extremely restrictive, expected value has served an enormous variety of business (and other, less respectable) gamblers for more than 300 years. Its applicability is most defensible for choices, or ventures, whose individual outcomes are small in relation to the decision maker's total resources; insurance companies and gambling casinos are classical areas of the application of the expected value concept.

Strictly speaking, a gamble's expected value is simply its arithmetic mean, or *average* outcome, over a very large number of trials. For example, define a hypothetical investment, or gamble, in terms of a simple coin-tossing experiment where, if heads appears, the "investor" *receives* $1.00, and if tails appears he *pays* $1.00; further assume that the coins are fair, in the sense that either outcome is equally likely; it can then be concluded, both intuitively and mathematically, that the investment's, or gamble's, expected value will be exactly zero. Intuitively, of course, the investor expects to lose as much on unfavorable outcomes (tails) as he expects to win on favorable outcomes (heads), and to lose such a gamble (on the average) as often as he wins. Mathematically, we may summarize this, or any other gamble's expected value by weighting each *conditional outcome* by its *of probability occurrence* and summing over all possible outcomes. Defining V as the gamble's expected value, $pr(h)$ and $pr(t)$ as the probabilities that heads and tails, respectively, will occur, X_h and X_t as payments conditional on heads or tails occurring, and recalling from the terms of the gamble that

$$X_h = \$1.00$$
$$X_t = -\$1.00$$

and since the coin is "fair"

$$pr(h) = pr(t) = \tfrac{1}{2}$$

the gamble's expected value (from a single toss of the coin) may be calculated, simply, as

$$V = pr(h)\, X_h + pr(t)\, X_t$$
$$= \tfrac{1}{2}\, (\$1.00) + \tfrac{1}{2}\, (-\$1.00)$$
$$= \$.50 - \$.50 = 0$$

Such a calculation can be generalized to cover gambles having any number (n) of possible outcomes; by defining: $pr(i)$ as the probability that a particu-

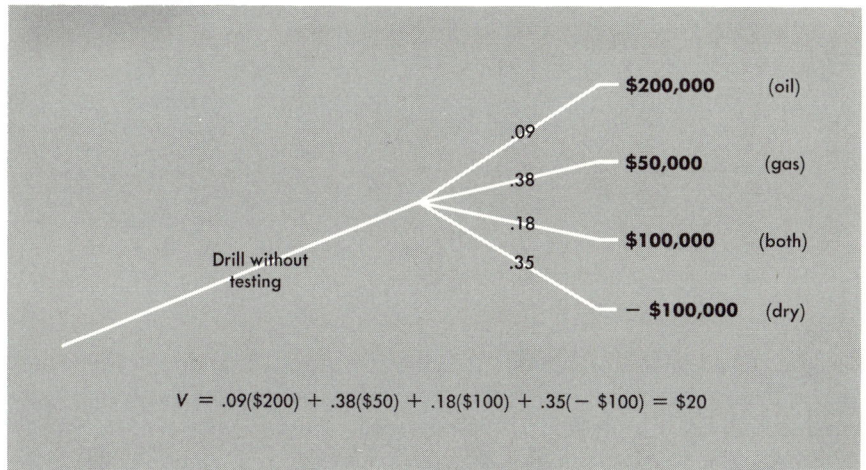

FIG. 5-12 Drill without testing.

lar outcome (i) will occur, X_i as the magnitude of the payment that results *if* outcome i occurs, and V, again, as the gamble's expected value, and writing

$$V = pr(1)X_1 + pr(2)X_2 + \ldots + pr(n)X_n$$

A *calculation* such as this, of course, is not itself a basis for acting, unless the decision maker considers it a sufficiently *complete* description of each venture's desirability to serve as an unambiguous basis for choice between alternative gambles. In particular, an expected value calculation, summarizing the payment to be expected on the average from a particular type of gamble over a large number of trials, is not likely to be sufficiently informative unless the type of gamble to which it is attached is sufficiently small *in relation to the decision maker's total resources* to insure that a large number of such gambles can, in fact, be undertaken. Thus, the fact that insurance companies and gambling casinos *are* able to assume *hundreds of thousands* of comparable risks virtually guarantees that such institutions may expect to actually obtain the long-run average or expected values provided by their investments.[5]

Jones, too, may consider the magnitude of his, say, $2,000,000-$3,000,000 annual exploration budget to be sufficiently large *relative to* the $100,000 cost of any particular dry hole to justify the use of expected

---

[5] This holds true barring war, pestilence or civil disorder for insurance companies or the development of systems to "beat the dealer" (e.g. by M.I.T.-trained gamblers). See E. O. Thorp's *Beat the Dealer: A Winning Strategy for the Game of 21*, rev. ed. (New York: Random House, Inc., 1962), 1966.

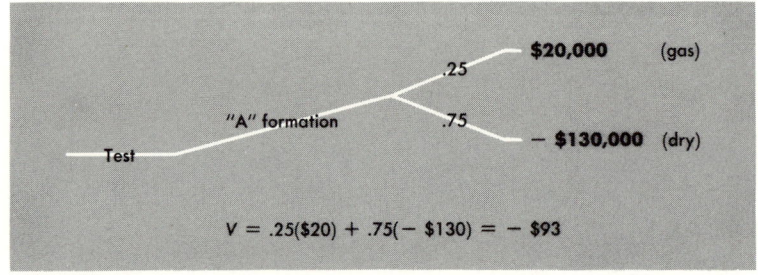

FIG. 5-13 Terminal drilling gamble: "A" formation.

value for choice between alternative drilling ventures. In short, he, too, may consider bankruptcy to be sufficiently remote from a foreseeable string of unfavorable outcomes to permit the attainment of long-run *expected returns*.

If so, Jones' observation that approximately 9 percent of the wells drilled (without testing) in this vicinity yielded oil; 38 percent brought in gas; 18 percent obtained both oil and gas; while 35 percent were dry;[6] may be applied, as in Fig. 5-12, to payouts for each outcome to produce an *expected monetary* value exactly equal to his previous $20,000 direct assessment of the gamble's "equivalent, certain value" to the firm.

Similar exercises clearly are possible for each of the other drilling gambles embedded in Jones' original decision tree. As three of the four wells actually drilled on "A" formations turned out to be dry, while the fourth yielded a gas pool, probabilities of ¾ and ¼ (or .75 and .25, respectively) may be attached to these outcomes (*if* they accurately reflect

[6] A careful reader may note that these percentages do not follow directly from the distribution of outcomes for the 70 wells already drilled on the field in question, but are adjusted to reflect an *assumption* that 6 of the 8 "A" formation holes *not drilled* after seismic testing would have turned out to be dry, while 2 would have contained gas pools, following the (3 dry, 1 gas) distribution of outcomes from the 4 "A" formations actually drilled.

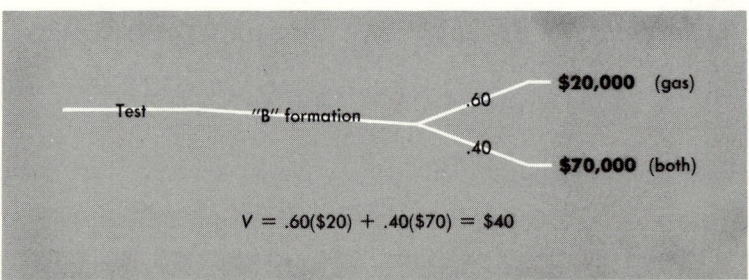

FIG. 5-14 Terminal drilling gamble: "B" formation.

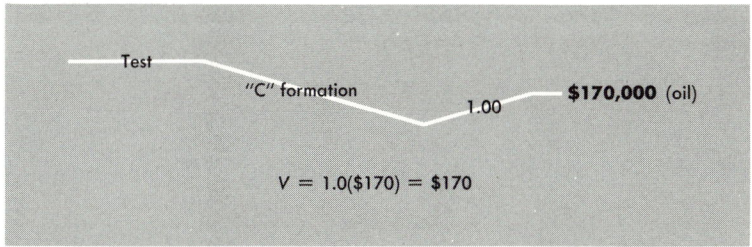

FIG. 5-15 Terminal drilling gamble; "C" formation.

Jones' subjective view of their relative likelihood) to yield an expected monetary value of −$93,000 for this (exceedingly unattractive) drilling gamble. Schematically, these calculations are summarized in Fig. 5-13.

Recalling that nine of the fifteen wells drilled on type "B" formations yielded gas pools, while each of the other six brought in combination oil and gas wells, Jones' expected value of $40,000 for wells on "B" formations can be derived with equal ease, as in Fig. 5-14.

And finally, if the discovery of a "C" type formation is considered tantamount to the imminent discovery of oil, an expected value of $170,000 for such a drilling opportunity will be assured, as in Fig. 5-15. Again, it should be emphasized that Jones' use of historical relative frequencies in making probability assessments, although pedagogically convenient, is not logically necessary. All that is necessary for Jones' purpose (or ours) is that the probabilities assigned accurately reflect the decision maker's views; whether or not they also correspond closely to historical frequencies is of relatively little interest.

Should we accept Jones' probability assessments as stated, and treat expected values for each terminal drilling opportunity as the gamble's *certainty equivalents*, several options can be quickly eliminated: such as "Drill, if an 'A' formation is discovered"; or "Abandon, if 'B' or 'C' formations are discovered," as before. Jones' original decision tree can thereby be reduced to the considerably simpler "equivalent" tree originally summarized in Fig. 5-9.

Jones also knows that 12 of the 30 seismic tests already performed on this field have yielded type "A" formations, 15 have indicated "B" formations, and 3 "C" formations. Should he accept these as accurate estimates of their relative chances of occurrence on the present tract, probability assessments of $12/30 = .4$, $15/30 = .5$, and $3/30 = .1$ for type "A," "B," and "C" outcomes, respectively, may be assigned. Employing these assessments to "roll back" Fig. 5-16's "Test" alternative to its source, a single, unambiguous $25,000 expected value is obtained.

The final result, predictably, is identical to that obtained by direct assessment in Fig. 5-11, and Jones, as before, is assumed to prefer a seismic test, whose expected value is $25,000, to either the drill-without-testing or sell options, whose expected values are $20,000 and $15,000, respectively.

By now, perhaps, the reader may be justifiably suspicious. Is it coincidental that Jones' directly assessed "certainty equivalents" are identical (except for a single instance of rounding) to calculated expected values or did expected values precede the certainty equivalents? The answer, in all honesty, must be that expected values did probably come first, for two reasons:

1. Because laboratory and teaching experience both have shown that direct assessments on an item-by-item basis of gambles no more complicated than those considered here are extremely difficult without the aid of some sort of formal criterion; and
2. Because untrained decision makers (including Mr. Jones) virtually always seize on expected values as a means of evaluating uncertain gambles, as soon as they are introduced to the certainty equivalence idea.

RISK PREFERENCE AND VALUATION

The fact that Jones is comfortable with use of expected values "in the large" does not guarantee, however, that he also will be happy with it "in the small." He may, for example, be entirely satisfied that expected value insures choices under uncertainty that are:

1. Consistent [7]
2. Transitive [8]
3. Decomposable [9]

and yet be dissatisfied by many of the specific choices that follow from its direct application.

To illustrate, engage in a little introspection. Suppose an experimenter were to offer *you* a simple bet, based on the toss of a coin, whose equally likely outcomes are ± $1.00, i.e., if heads occurs you win $1.00, if tails occurs you lose $1.00. An expected value calculation is likely to quickly reinforce your instinctive belief that the opportunity to take such a bet is

---

[7] Where consistency is defined either in terms of fundamental axioms (such as, if A is more valuable than B, A will be preferred to B), or in temporal terms (as, for example, if A is more valuable than B, when once seen, it also will be more valuable when next seen—unless something occurs to change the decision maker's situation and attitude toward risk).

[8] Where transitivity may be defined roughly as satisfying the condition that if A is preferred to B, and B to C, then A is also preferred to C.

[9] Decomposability is satisfied if complex gambles whose initial outcomes specify only contingent future gambles (such as "seismic test") can be decomposed into logically equivalent simple gambles whose outcomes are the *certain* receipt of particular consequences; such as a specified cash payment.

UNCERTAINTY

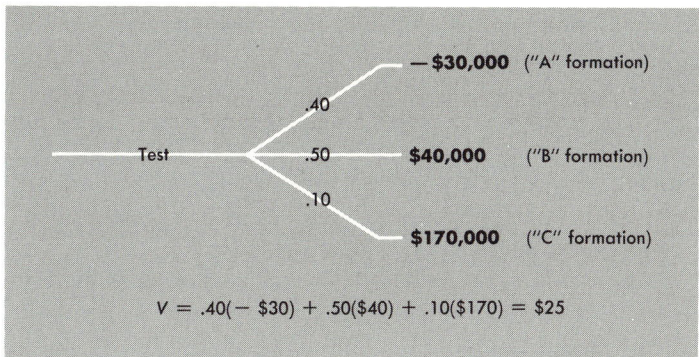

FIG. 5-16 Final terminal gamble: seismic test alternative.

absolutely worthless; or that its *equivalent, certain* value, like its expected value, is exactly zero:

$$V = \tfrac{1}{2}(\$1.00) + \tfrac{1}{2}(-\$1.00) = 0.0.$$

Invoking the emotionally sterile atmosphere of a "laboratory experiment" to nullify possible moral objections to or psychic pleasures from gambling *per se,* assume for the moment that you concur with the criterion's conclusion that such a gamble's economic value *is* zero; and express your *indifference* toward the bet either by a visible yawn or a shrug of the shoulders as the offer is made; or by a counter offer to flip another coin as your criterion for accepting or rejecting the bet.

Now let us suppose the experimenter is sufficiently determined and well-financed to press on, by offering you another gamble that is identical in every respect, except for the magnitude of its stakes; e.g., a gamble whose (equally likely) outcomes are ± $10.00. Again the experiment's expected value will be exactly zero; for

$$V = \tfrac{1}{2}(\$10.00) + \tfrac{1}{2}(-\$10.00) = 0.0.$$

Should you again shrug your shoulders in indifference, implying your agreement with the expected value criterion's assertion that the gamble's *value* to you is zero; the experimenter can, simply, *further increase* the bet's (symmetric) payoffs to ± $1,000; or if necessary to ± $100,000; *until finally he makes his point.* That point is that despite the fact that any gamble whose equally likely outcomes are *symmetrical* will have an *expected value* of zero, your own assessment of the relative importance of gaining or losing a particular quantity of money is not likely to be symmetrical as larger and larger potential gains (and losses) are considered. This assertion, although rather obvious intuitively (to most persons), strikes at the heart of most individuals' faith in an expected value criterion; for it asserts that, over a *broad range* of possible monetary outcomes, a gamble's *expected value* will not necessarily be its *equivalent, certain value* to any specific person like yourself, or Mr. Jones, or most other decision makers under uncertainty.

To permit rational choice under uncertainty, then, some mechanism for summarizing a decision maker's attitude toward the types of risks encountered, in a way that permits their decomposition and comparison, is necessary. An extremely simple way of obtaining such a transformation can best be developed, perhaps, through another example.

Let us invent a second decision maker who, unlike Mr. Jones, does not deal in millions of dollars, and who is averse to risk, even where relatively small amounts of money are involved. Let us call him Mr. Smith (of course), and assume that he is considering two alternative gambles; one involving an 80 percent chance at $60 with a complementary chance at $10; the other promising a 20 percent chance at $90 with an 80 percent chance at $40, as summarized in Table 5-1.

Table 5-1 SMITH'S OPPORTUNITY SET

Venture 1		Venture 2	
Probability	Outcome	Probability	Outcome
.8	$60	.2	$90
.2	$10	.8	$40

Let us assume that each gamble is available to Mr. Smith and that his problem is to determine which is the better, or even more explicitly, how much either is worth?

A little arithmetic will quickly verify that both gambles have an expected value of exactly $50. If Smith considers the risks involved to be nontrivial, however, expected values will be poor measures of actual values, or certainty equivalents, from his point of view.

Let us assume, however, that Smith can be induced to answer a series of hypothetical (although related) questions about the value to himself of a set of simple *reference gambles* involving payments that span the range of consequences faced by him in this, and other decisions, under uncertainty. Specifically, let us assume that Smith is willing and able to calibrate his *preferences for risk* in terms of $100 and $0.0 *reference consequences* for simple, two-outcome experiments, by stating that a gamble promising a 90 percent chance, q, at $100 with a complementary, $1 - q$, 10 percent chance at $0.0 would be worth, say $78 to him; that a similar gamble offering an 80 percent chance, at a $100 payment (again with a complementary chance, now 20 percent, at $0.0) would be worth only $63, and so forth for a number of similar reference gambles. As the probability of a successful outcome approaches either unity or zero, uncertainty about the gamble's outcome disappears by definition: approching $100 for certain as the probability, q, goes to 1.0 insuring a favorable outcome, and $0.0 *for certain* as q approaches zero, guaranteeing an unfavorable outcome. Our Mr. Smith or any other decision maker, of course, would pay $100 or $0.0 for either "sure thing," depending on which is available. Say that Smith's *certainty equivalents* for these gambles are as summarized in Table 5-2, and illustrated graphically by the solid, concave downward curve in Fig. 5-17.

Table 5-2 CERTAINTY EQUIVALENTS TO SMITH
FOR SIMPLE REFERENCE GAMBLES

Involving $100 and $0.0 Payments

Porbability of receiving $100	Probability of receiving $0.0	Certainty Equivalents
q	1 — q	$
1.0	.0	100
.9	.1	78
.8	.2	63
.7	.3	51
.6	.4	41
.5	.5	32
.4	.6	24
.3	.7	17
.2	.8	11
.1	.9	5
.0	1.0	0

Were Smith *not* risk averse—were he willing to rely on averages to value any gamble at its actuarial or mathematical expectation—his certainty equivalent for any gamble would be identical to its expected value, and his risk preference function in Fig. 5-17 would be expressed by the dotted straight line, rather than the solid, concave downward curve derived earlier. Furthermore, the greater our decision maker's degree of risk aversion, the less he will pay for a particular gamble, and the greater will be the degree of curvature displayed by his risk preference function. Measuring the difference between a gamble's expected value and its certainty equivalent, we can see that the risk premium required to induce Smith to accept a risky venture such as the $q = .6$ reference gamble in Fig. 5-17 is substantial, amounting to $19 = $60 − $41, or nearly one-third of the opportunity's expected value.

But, one should note that assessments of this sort, summarizing a decision maker's attitude toward risk can be repeated any number of times, spaced over as fine or as broad an interval as desired, and could run in either direction; that is, our Mr. Smith could be asked to assess *either* "how much he would be willing to pay for a particular reference gamble (characterized, say, by a .7 chance at $100)?" or "how large the probability of winning ($100) would have to be for such a gamble to be worth $50 to him?" In either case, uncertain gambles are calibrated in terms of *equivalent certain payments,* and certain payments in terms of *equivalent reference gambles.*

Our purpose in calibrating the decision maker's risk preferences in this

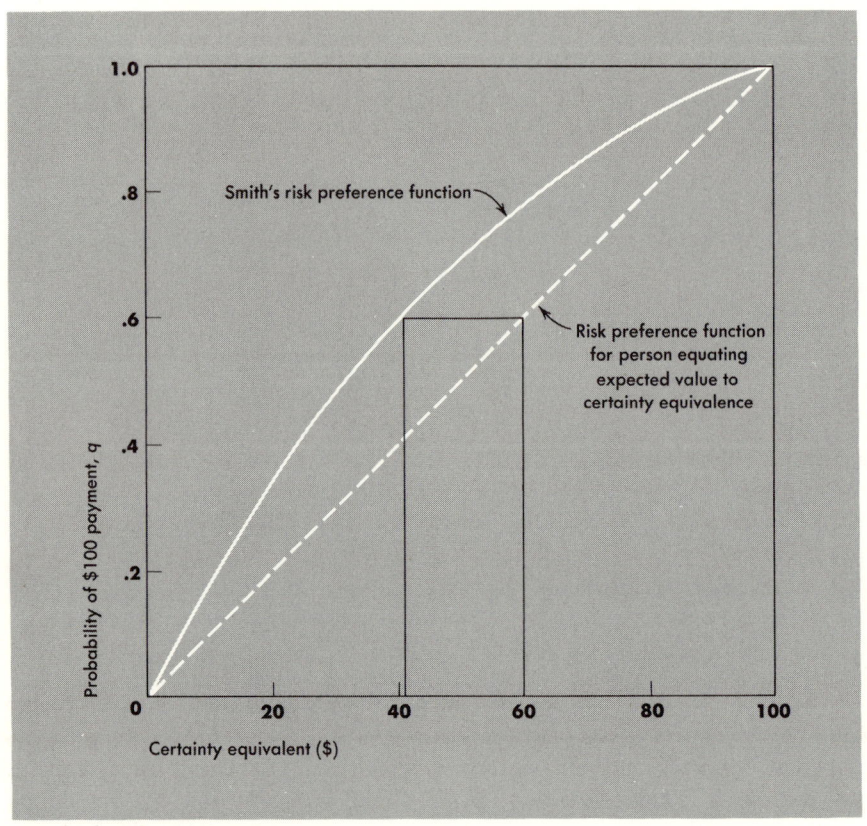

FIG. 5-17 Risk preference functions relating certainty equivalents to simple reference gambles involving $100 and $0.0 payments.

fashion, however, is not to evaluate Smith's subjective liking for *certain* quantities of money, or even to rank and distinguish between reference gambles, or to display risk preferences graphically. Instead, it is to obtain a capability of comparing, ranking, and evaluating quite *dissimilar gambles,* whose only common characteristics are that all potential consequences lie within the interval spanned by the calibrating reference gambles and their consequences.

Let us return, therefore, to Smith's original (nonreference) gambles and consider the manner in which a risk preference function, such as Fig. 5-17, could assist in their evaluation. Consider initially the first of the ventures whose payments and associated probabilities are summarized in Table 5-1, and note at the outset that the conditional $60 outcome is *equivalent in value* to the reference gamble offering chances $q = .78$ at $100 and $(1 - q) = .22$ at 0.0. Similarly, the venture's $10 conditional payment can be seen to be *equivalent in value* to the reference gamble offering $100 with

UNCERTAINTY

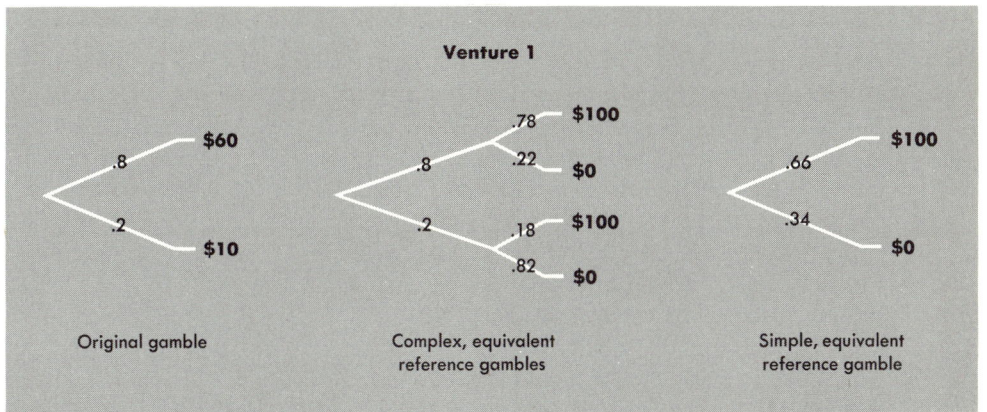

FIG. 5-18 Decomposition and risk evaluation: venture 1.

probability $q = .18$ and $0.0 with probability $(1 - q) = .82$. Stop here, and be sure these comparisons are fully understood, for they are essential to everything that follows.

Should Smith *mean* it when he says that the reference gambles and certainty equivalents summarized in Table 5-2 and Fig. 5-17 are in fact *equivalent in value* to each other; then the gamble summarized as Venture 1 in Table 5-1 and as the left-hand diagram in Fig. 5-18 also can be seen to be *entirely equivalent* to the corresponding *pair of reference gambles* diagrammed in the figure's middle panel; for the transformation involves nothing more than a one-for-one substitution of *equivalent* reference gambles for $60 and $10 conditional payments. The next step, of course, is entirely

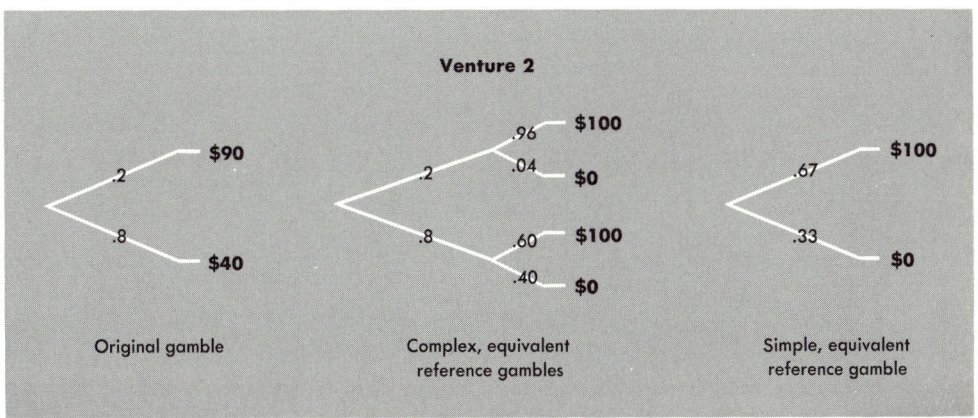

FIG. 5-19 Decomposition and risk evaluation: venture 2.

mechanical; for once all terminal payments are either $100 or $0.0 reference consequences, like terms can be collected, and the complex pair of reference gambles in the figure's middle panel can be reduced to the *logically identical* simple reference gamble in its right-hand panel. All three of these entirely equivalent gambles, then, are identical in value to the (right-hand) "simple reference gamble" offering $q = .66$ at a favorable, $100 outcome. By returning to Smith's risk preference function in Fig. 5-17, of course, we also may conclude that each is equivalent in value to the certain receipt of $46 in cash.

Through an identical sequence of steps, Smith's second venture first can be transcribed from Table 5-1 to the left-hand panel of Fig. 5-19; second, decomposed by translating $90 and $40 certain payments into $q = .96$ and $q = .60$ equivalent reference gambles (in the figure's middle panel); and finally, like terms may be collected to reduce this pair of reference gambles to the *simple* reference gamble on Fig. 5-19's right-hand side.

Smith now has a choice of criteria for evaluating and ranking his original pair of uncertain ventures. He may simply characterize each by the simple reference gamble to which it is equivalent in value; or he may return to Fig. 5-17's risk preference function to convert these equivalent reference gambles into equivalent, *certain* sums of money. In either case his result will be the same, for the reference gamble offering a larger probability of obtaining the favorable outcome, of course, also will possess the larger certainty equivalent, and vice versa. In this case, Venture 2, yielding an equivalent reference gamble characterized by $q = .67$ at the favorable outcome, and a certainty equivalent of $48, edges out Venture 1's $q = .66$ and $46.50 measures of merit by a proverbial "eyelash."

A structure of this magnitude for so simple a problem, of course, would be silly. Our decision maker could provide two direct assessments for his original gambles much more easily than he could the dozen or so direct assessments built into Fig. 5-17's risk preference function, and the sequence of calculations that follows in the problem's formal solution. It is true, of course, that without the aid of such a procedure he may on occasion provide inconsistent direct assessments, leading to formally "incorrect" solutions. Still, the analytical effort incurred in this instance to avoid the potential $1.50 cost of an incorrect choice, can be described only as excessive.

As one passes from very simple illustrative examples to more realistic problems such as Jones', however, one notices first of all that the stakes become substantially larger; second, that the problem's size tends to grow considerably; and third, that our ability to reduce complex reference gambles to equivalent simple reference gambles by straightforward expected value operations remains unimpaired, and becomes exceedingly efficient computationally. Recall, for example, that Smith's $q = .66$ probability of obtaining the favorable outcome from his first venture's equivalent, simple reference gamble can be calculated, simply, by summing the probability of success from each terminal reference gamble *should it be* obtained, times the probability *that it will in fact be* obtained, or numerically (from Fig. 5-18's middle panel) as,

$$q = .8(.78) + .2(.18) = .66.$$

Similarly, Venture 2's complex reference gamble can be reduced to the probability of success from an equivalent simple reference gamble, by summing

$$q = .2(.96) + .8(.60) = .67$$

to obtain the desired measure of merit. Once a decision problem has been structured and the decision maker's risk preference function is in hand, then, no matter how complex the problem may be, the decision maker's active participation no longer is required. He may safely retire to a golf course while either an underpaid analyst or a dumb computer completes the purely arithmetic aspects of evaluating his problem.

EVALUATION OF STRATEGIES

Should our decision maker be willing and able to diagram his problem's logical structure and provide the probability assessments and risk preferences needed for its solution, the procedures illustrated above are not only feasible but can be shown to lead to optimal results.

Twixt most theoretical concepts and their operational implementation, however, there generally exists a substantial number of potential "slips." Suppose the outcome of a sequence such as "Drill: Strike Oil," leads not to the *certain* receipt of *exactly* $200,000, but instead to an uncertain outcome whose *expected* value is $200,000, and whose *exact* value depends on the quantity and quality of the oil discovered, the pool's depth and geological formation, etc. In short, suppose that each of our decision tree's existing terminal *values* is replaced by a terminal *fork*; or worse, by a *time sequence* of uncertain outcomes for each of an uncertain number of future time periods.

Or assume that instead of being President, Chief Executive Officer, and virtual owner of the XYZ Wildcat Company, Jones is Assistant Regional Manager for Wildcatting Operations in the Western Texas Regional Branch Office of the Mammoth International Oil Corporation. The company, perhaps, is publicly owned; has Corporate headquarters in Europe; United States headquarters in New York City; and a chain of command that stretches through its Southern Regional headquarters in St. Louis, its Texas Regional Office in Houston, to Jones in the (Lubbock) Western Texas Regional Branch Office. Whose risk preferences should Jones use in evaluating this, or any other "Drill," "Test" or "Sell" opportunities he may encounter: his own? his Regional Manager's (and, if so, the one from Lubbock, Houston, St. Louis or New York)? the Corporate Exploration Manager's? the Corporate President's? or the Amsterdam Stock Exchange's?

Jones, clearly, may have some problems on his hands whose solutions are far from obvious. The fact that these problems are operational rather than conceptual does not in any way diminish their importance. Decisions under uncertainty involving corporate resources and terminal gambles whose outcomes are too numerous to diagram, are encountered and resolved every day, with or without the assistance of logically impregnable analytical tools. The fact that an increasing number of these problems are yielding to systematic analysis is a tribute to the emerging maturity of managerial sciences as a discipline, as well as to the increasing number and sophistication of its practitioners.

The existence of imprecisely defined corporate risk preferences and gambles containing innumerable outcomes, however, requires some modifications to the approach outlined above. One very common and generally effective response consists of very precise analyses of the *distribution of possible outcomes* from each of a relatively small number of a decision problem's *complete strategies;* where each strategy contains a *full* description of the decision maker's response to *all possible contingencies* that may arise between his initial (or current) and terminal positions.

Jones' original drilling problem provides an altogether typical example. Any attempt to enumerate its embedded complete strategies would quickly turn up two or three that are entirely sensible and that may well turn out to be serious competitors for the decision maker's final choice, such as,

1. Sell option,
2. Drill without testing,
3. Test and: if "A" abandon, if "B" or "C" drill,

while any of a large number of alternative strategies (involving decisions to drill on "A" formations, or abandon "C" formations, for example) can be ruled out without formal (or even serious) consideration.

Once a relatively small number of basically attractive strategies has been selected for intensive analysis, terminal values and probabilistic information alone are needed to derive and display the *distribution* of possible monetary outcomes anticipated from each. From a direct examination of the terminal event fork corresponding to Jones' "Drill Without Testing" gamble, for example, an assessment of the decision maker's "chance" of receiving each possible outcome, should he adopt the strategy, can be derived easily and displayed as the probability distribution in Fig. 5-20a. For this very simple strategy, of course, each monetary outcome can be linked directly to a single branch of the basic gamble's terminal event fork. Jones' assessment of a 35 percent chance of losing $100,000 on such a venture corresponds directly to

UNCERTAINTY

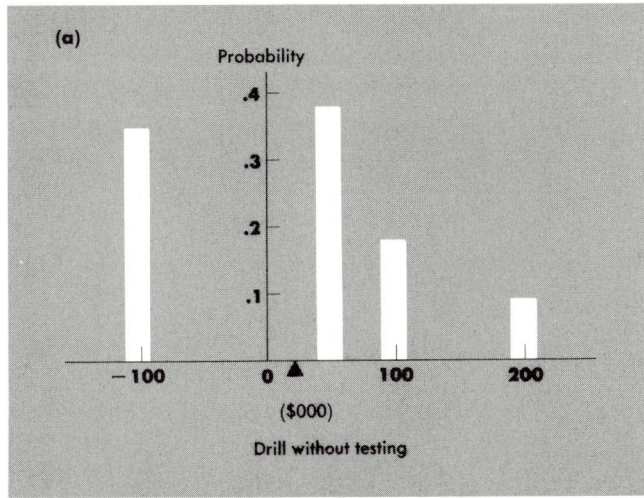

FIG. 5-20a Distribution of outcomes from alternative strategies.

his views of the probability of obtaining a dry hole. Similarly, his assessments of 38 percent, 18 percent and 9 percent chances of receiving $50,000, $100,000 and $200,000 correspond uniquely to his perceptions of the respective probabilities of locating "Gas," "both Oil and Gas," or "Oil alone" from a well "Drilled Without Testing" on this location.

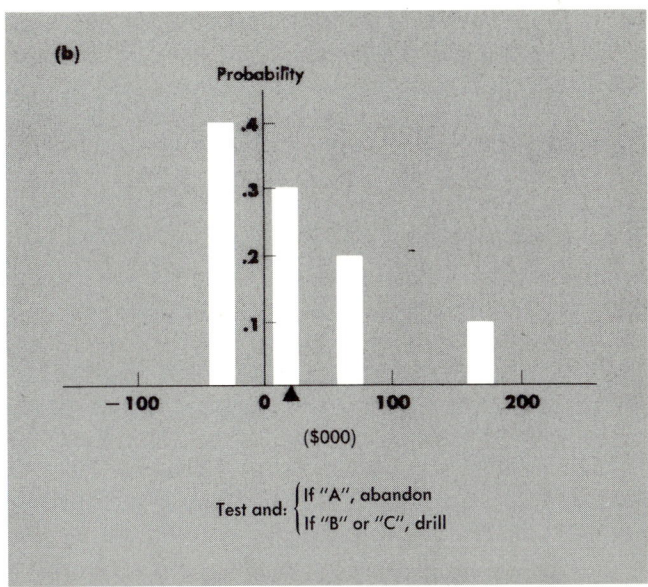

FIG. 5-20b

97

Somewhat greater effort is required to trace through those portions of the decision tree corresponding to our decision maker's more complex "Test and if 'A' abandon; if 'B' or 'C' drill" strategy, but this effort, too, can be summarized in some detail as in Table 5-3 and lead to the distribution of possible monetary outcomes in columns 6 and 7 of the table, displayed visually as the frequency distribution in Fig. 5-20b.

Table 5-3 DISTRIBUTION OF OUTCOMES, "TEST AND…"ALTERNATIVES

Test Outcome	Probability	Act	Drill Outcome	Probability	Value Outcome	Compound Probability†
(1)	(2)	(3)	(4)	(5)	(6)	(7)
"A"	.4	Abandon		1.0	—$30,000	.4×1.0= .4
		Gas		.6	$20,000	.5× .6= .3
"B"	.5	Drill				
		Combination		.4	$70,000	.5× .4= .2
"C"	.1	Drill	Oil	1.0	$170,000	.1×1.0= .1

† Calculated as the product of columns 2 and 5.

Jones' third and final strategy, "Sell Option," of course, can be characterized by the most simple of all probability distributions, one whose entire mass is centered (with probability = 1.0 in Fig. 5-20c) on its *only possible outcome,* the *certain* receipt of $15,000.

The essential character of Jones' three "serious alternatives" is displayed graphically and quite dramatically by Fig. 5-20's frequency distributions. By virtually eliminating the probability of drilling to discover a "Dry Hole," Jone's "Test and . . ." alternative shifts the mass of his most unfavorable outcome from a "Drill Without Testing" gamble's possible $100,000 loss to the considerably more modest $30,000 loss, i.e., from the cost of *drilling* on an unproductive site to the cost of discovering the location's barrenness by conducting a seismic *test.* Seismic testing, of course, does not confer an unmixed blessing, for by adding its costs to those of drilling on favorable sites, net payoffs from successful wells are reduced (by exactly $30,000) from their values under a more venturesome "Drill Without Testing" strategy (compare Figs. 5-20a and 5-20b). Which gamble is the more attractive depends, of course, finally and inescapably on Jones' (or his Branch Manager's or his Company's . . .) preferences between the two gambles, with Fig. 5-20c's $15,000 "sure thing" waiting in the wings.

The point of translating our problem's "net present values" and "probabilities of obtaining same" from a decision tree format, such as Fig. 5-1's, to Fig. 5-20's frequency distributions may seem a little obscure; for no clear logical benefits are obtained from so mechanical an operation. All that changes is the point at which the decision maker's risk preferences are brought to bear on the problem. Instead of introducing these preferences

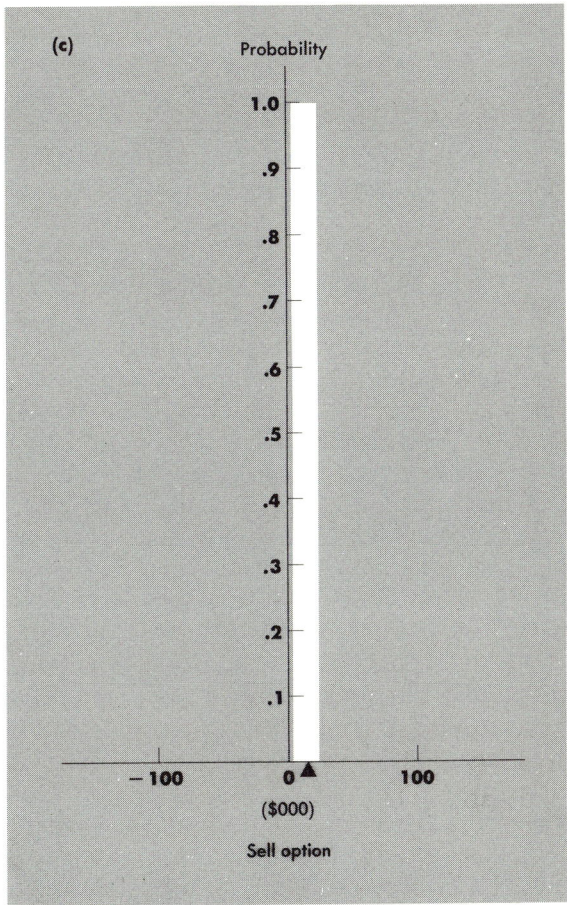

FIG. 5-20c

from the beginning to continuously eliminate less desirable alternatives—and in the process, to continuously narrow the set of strategies actively considered—final choice is postponed until the full distribution of possible outcomes for a limited number of "realistic alternatives" has been developed.

Should a decision problem closely resemble Jones', there would in fact be little purpose to such a transformation. True, the number of points at which subjective preferences must be brought to bear on the problem would be reduced. So also would the intuitive character of a problem's basic choices be highlighted by visual displays such as Fig. 5-20's frequency distributions. As long as a decision problem may safely be described in a *single period context,* however, there is really no need to reduce the number of occasions on which subjective preferences are employed, for such assessments can be derived easily from the decision maker's previously specified risk preference function. Similarly, the manner in which information is displayed should not be of overriding importance. Any displays desired may be developed after the fact, either by a computer, or by an analyst. Jones' primary task, however, is not to *display* information, but to *decide* on sensible courses of action. And for this purpose, evaluation by rollback can guarantee a *fully optimal* decision, while the evaluation of complete strategies can guarantee only that the best of strategies actually considered will be selected. This set, of course, may or may not contain the best available course of action.

Once a gamble's "single period, immediate resolution of uncertainty" character is lost, however, a decision maker's ability to diagram decision problems to a common time horizon, systematically calibrate risk preferences for gambles resolved at that point in time, and as a result "roll back" decision trees to optimal courses of action (other than by unaided, direct assessment) is lost. In a formal sense, the problem cannot be solved today. Multiple period decisions under uncertainty are literally on the frontiers of management science. In a practical sense, however, an analyst provided with a measure of his firm's cost of capital is able to calculate the present value, contribution to net worth, equivalent annual return, or any other capital budgeting measure of merit *for a particular operating cash flow*. By doing so repetitively, under different assumptions about uncertain future developments (such as the depth at which oil might be discovered, the prices at which crude could be sold during each future time period, etc.), where these assumptions are chosen according to frequencies that accurately reflect the decision maker's assessment of their relative likelihoods, one may effectively merge the tools of simulation, capital budgeting and risk analysis to build up a complete *distribution of possible outcomes* for any strategy desired. By relying on simulation to provide needed computational power, capital budgeting to handle differences in the time profile of cash flows, and the concepts of certainty equivalence, or simply risk evaluation developed in this chapter, we arrive simultaneously at one of the most active frontiers of the discipline, and the end of our *introduction* to managerial economics as it exists today.

Postscript

CHAPTER SIX

In this book an attempt has been made to introduce the student to certain economic concepts that are tenderly used for analyzing the problems confronted by business managements. For this purpose the *function of management* has been defined, admittedly quite narrowly, as that of marshalling and converting supplies of various capital assets, as well as types of labor and materials, into products or services which are to be sold so as to maximize the profits or the net present value of those capital assets committed to the business firm.

As noted at several places in the text, several simplifications lurk behind all this. At a most basic level, many would dispute the primacy, let alone exclusive pursuit, of the profit motive. At a minimum, the profit motive may be regulated or constrained, as in the case of the electric utility pricing problem discussed in Chapter Two. More generally, it has been argued that modern day business corporations often serve many masters besides their stockholders, such as laboring groups, the local communities where plants and offices are located, or some broadly construed national or social interest. Management's concerns, moreover, may not always parallel those of the owners in any complete or direct sense. Nevertheless, it does simplify analytical problems to ignore these complications, and simplification after all, lies at the very heart of analysis.[1]

A very real question remains, though, of how much simplification is justified. Even within the context of profit maximization

---

[1] For a treatment of business decisions that to a considerable extent eschews such simplification see K. J. Cohen and R. M. Cyert, *Theory of the Firm: Resource Allocation in a Market Economy* (Englewood Cliffs, N.J.: Prentice-Hall, Inc., 1965), pp. 303-384.

some of the analytical procedures presented in this volume could be deemed naive. For example, the question was posed (at the end of Chapter Four), but never really answered, of how to define in strict terms who really owns a firm's assets or, if ownership is mixed, as it usually is, for whose assets are values to be maximized. Conceptually, profit maximization seems best applied to those assets irrevocably committed to the enterprises of the firm, and which are rewarded for this commitment by a *residual* claim on returns realized by the firm. Of course, in a modern market economy with well-developed and complex financial institutions, the extent to which a particular financial instrument is a residual or non-residual claimant on business returns can be a matter of degree. These complexities have simply been ignored in most of the analyses presented. In general, our treatment of corporation or business finance, and all attendant institutional and legal questions, has been marked by omission or the crudest of simplifications.

Omission or over-simplification also characterizes our discussions of the firm as an organizational entity.[2] To some extent these oversights were justified by considerations of professional competence and specialization. While economists and economic concepts might provide some limited insight into how a business should or does organize itself internally, such insights are not commonly stressed within the economics literature. They are not, moreover, particularly essential to understanding or using the tools of economic analysis for making managerial decisions.

Only limited attention has been given also to the relationship of the firm to its external environment. For example, there has been little discussion of how anti-trust laws, government safety or pricing regulations, federal regulatory institutions or community environment might condition or constrain business decisions. Nor, to any great extent, has there been any discussion of how different kinds of external market conditions—denoted by economists by such terms as "monopoly" or "oligopoly" or "monopolistic competition"—might condition business decisions and reactions. These have been excluded not because they are irrelevant to business decisions; indeed they are often most relevant. Rather, their exclusion was directed by simple limitations on space and the fact that to some considerable extent these questions have been addressed elsewhere in this series.[3]

Nor does this volume catalog all of the concepts and tools which economists have developed and which might be deemed potentially useful for making business decisions. The most notorious such omission is the lack of any real discussion of so-called simulation techniques and related systems analyses.[4] Increasingly, business decisions, and the teaching of managerial

---

[2] For such a discussion see H. A. Simon, *The New Science of Management Decision* (New York: Harper & Row, Publishers, 1960).

[3] Richard Caves, *American Industry: Structure, Conduct, Performance,* in this series, 1964.

[4] Systems analysis, a somewhat amorphous term, is not, however, completely synonymous or coincident with computer simulations. For a good introduction to

practice, involve the use of what are called simulation or system models as operated on large electronic calculators.[5] In essence, these computer models are nothing more (nor less!) than quite complex and large scale models designed to emulate or simulate the more relevant characteristics of how business systems behave. Electronic calculators are employed for the simple reason that the models are usually too complex to be handled by manual procedures. The interdependencies, the feed-backs and the non-linearities seemingly required for reasonably realistic models are often beyond what can be easily analyzed without a computer.

Simulation models can be used for analyzing a wide variety of business problems, for example, to trace out the more important implications of various marketing, product innovation, investment and other developmental strategies. Simulations are especially helpful in analyzing new procedures or developments that might be expected to influence operations throughout the business firm, that is have *system-wide effects*. By varying the assumptions built into a model, the sensitivity of the system to different possibilities can be evaluated. Such *sensitivity analyses* are relatively easy to perform once the model has been computerized.

By introducing what is called man-machine interaction computer models can also be employed to determine possible responses which business decisions might elicit from competitors, government or other persons whose actions might impinge upon a business firm's activities or realizations. Man-machine interaction essentially involves creating a game wherein the human players take actions in response to situations as defined or created by the computer model and the actions of other players.

Interactions between businesses and their exterior environments may also be analyzed by using other tools of economic analyses not discussed in this volume. The most important of these comprise what is called the "theory of games." That theory can be used, for example, to provide insight into how firms act in a context of different external market circumstances, such as monopoly or oligopoly.[6] The theory of games also provides an alternative approach to analyzing particular types of business decisions under conditions of uncertainty—specifically when the decision maker's uncertainty arises not from random events, whose probable occurrence does not depend on his own decisions, but from the conscious reactions of others, especially competitors, to those decisions.

To a considerable extent, the central theme of this book has been that,

---

systems analysis see R. A. Johnson, F. E. Kost, and J. E. Rosenzweig, *The Theory and Management of Systems* (New York: McGraw-Hill Book Company, 1963).

[5] The classic introduction to systems modelling as applied to business decision is J. W. Forrester, *Industrial Dynamics* (Cambridge, Mass.: The M.I.T. Press, and New York: John Wiley & Sons, Inc., 1961).

[6] For a comprehensive treatment of these matters see Martin Shubik, *Strategy and Market Structure: Competition, Oligopoly, and the Theory of Games* (New York: John Wiley & Sons, Inc., 1959).

for those involved in management, tradeoffs almost invariably exist and must be confronted. As the reader of this postscript can discern, this theme is a consideration in textbook writing as well. Tradeoffs exist between treating new subjects or extending and deepening the treatment of those already offered. As indicated at several points in the text, all of the discussions presented are considerably short of exhaustive. Specifically, depth has been sacrificed in order to make the reader aware of the pervasiveness of analytical problems in managerial practice and the possible wide variety of problems to which a few basic and highly general concepts can be applied.

Finally, perhaps a few words are needed to justify the relevance of all this, that is of managerial economics. But that is easily done. Improving the techniques of business management must be deemed useful as long as materialistic goals or economic development are of interest, if for no other reason than the quality of managerial decisions, both public and private, significantly influences the economic well being of a society.

Selected Readings

The literature on the general nature, character and objectives of business management is enormous and highly varied in content and treatment. Several of the most important references are given in the first footnote of Chapter One. To quickly acquire familiarity with a wide range of views on the nature of modern capitalism and management, three citations in that footnote deserve special attention: (1) A. Berle and G. Means, *The Modern Corporation and Private Property,* which is the classic, though controversial, statement on the relationships between ownership and control; (2) F. Machlup, "Theories of the Firm: Marginalist, Behavioral, Managerial," which represents a scholarly summary of the issues, albeit presented from the viewpoint of one somewhat partisan to the economist's conventional marginal analysis; and (3) R. M. Cyert and J. G. March, *A Behavioral Theory of the Firm,* which both summarizes and originates much of what is best in modern behavioral interpretations of business procedures.

For an introduction to managerial accounting, see C. L. Moore and R. J. Jaedicke, *Managerial Accounting* (Cincinnati, Ohio: South-Western Publishing, 1963). At a more intermediate level, with special emphasis on financial accounting, see H. Bierman, Jr., *Financial Accounting Theory* (New York: The Macmillan Company, 1965).

Almost any textbook on price theory will provide a good introduction to the marginalist concepts outlined in Chapter Two. Probably the single best source on advanced applications of marginalist concepts to practical pricing problems is *Marginal Cost Pricing in Practice* (Englewood Cliffs, N.J.: Prentice-Hall, Inc., 1964), edited by J. R. Nelson.

For an advanced and comprehensive treatment of inventory planning problems see G. Hadley and M. Whitin, *Analysis of Inventory Systems* (Englewood Cliffs, N.J.: Prentice-Hall, Inc., 1963). A highly suggestive and original treatment of the inventory problem as it relates to other aspects of managerial planning can be found in C. Holt, J. Muth, F. Modigliani, and H. A. Simon, *Planning Produc-*

tion, Inventories and Work Force (Englewood Cliffs, N.J.: Prentice-Hall, Inc., 1960).

For nontechnical introductory treatments of linear programming, see R. Dorfman, "Mathematical or 'Linear' Programming," *American Economic Review* (December 1953) and A. Henderson and R. Schlaifer, "Mathematical Programming," *Harvard Business Review* (May-June 1954). For more extensive, yet still basically nontechnical treatments, including duality, nonlinear and integer programming, see W. Baumol, *Economic Theory and Operations Analysis*, 2nd ed. (Englewood Cliffs, N.J.: Prentice-Hall, Inc., 1965), Chapter Five through Eight, and H. M. Weingartner, *Mathematical Programming and the Analysis of Capital Budgeting Problems* (Englewood Cliffs, N.J.: Prentice Hall, Inc., 1963 and Markham Publishing Co., 1967). For fuller, technical developments of linear programming methods, applications and implications, see G. Hadley, *Linear Programming* (Reading, Mass.: Addison-Wesley, 1962); R. Dorfman, P. A. Samuelson, and R. M. Solow, *Linear Programming and Economic Analysis* (New York: McGraw-Hill Book Company, 1958); and A. Charnes and W. W. Cooper, *Management Models and Industrial Applications of Linear Programming*, 2 volumes (New York: John Wiley & Sons, Inc., 1961).

Any list of references on capital budgeting should include (but need not be limited to) the following: J. Dean or H. M. Weingartner in *Capital Budgeting* (New York: Columbia University Press, 1951); G. D. Quirin, *The Capital Expenditure Decision* (New York: John Wiley & Sons, Inc., 1967); and E. Solomon, ed., *The Management of Corporate Capital* (New York: The Free Press of Glencoe, 1959).

For introductory treatments of the theory underlying business finance, see E. Solomon, *The Theory of Financial Management* (New York: Columbia University Press, 1963), and B. J. Moore, *An Introduction to the Theory of Finance* (New York: The Free Press of Glencoe, 1968). For more conventional treatments, see J. F. Weston and E. Brigham, *Managerial Finance*, 2nd ed. (New York: Holt, Rinehart and Winston, 1966) and J. C. VanHorne, *Financial Management and Policy* (Englewood Cliffs, N.J.: Prentice-Hall, Inc., 1968).

For an introduction to probability theory, see either T. R. Dyckman, S. Smidt, and A. K. McAdams, *Management Decision Making Under Uncertainty* (New York: The Macmillan Company, 1969), Chapters One through Eight; or S. Goldberg, *Probability: An Introduction* (Englewood Cliffs, N.J.: Prentice-Hall, Inc., 1960). For a more advanced treatment, see either W. Feller, *An Introduction to Probability Theory and Its Application,* 2 volumes (New York: John Wiley & Sons, 1966); or E. Parzen, *Modern Probability Theory and Its Applications* (New York: John Wiley & Sons, 1960). For an introduction to Statistical Decision Theory, see either I. D. J. Bross or T. R. Dyckman, S. Smidt and A. K. McAdams in *Design for Decision* (New York: The Macmillan Company, 1957), Chapters Nine through Seventeen; also R. Schlaifer, *Analysis of Decisions Under Uncertainty* (New York: McGraw-Hill Book Company, 1965). More advanced treatments include J. Pratt, H. Raiffa, and R. Schlaifer, *Introduction to Statistical Decision Theory* (New York: McGraw-Hill Book Company, 1965); and H. Raiffa and R. Schlaifer, *Applied Statisitcal Decision Theory* (Boston: Division of Research, Harvard Business School, 1961).

Appendix

Table 1 PRESENT VALUE OF $1

Periods of Payment	2%	4%	6%	8%	10%	12%	14%	15%	16%	18%	20%	25%	30%	35%	40%	45%	50%
1	0.980	0.962	0.943	0.926	0.909	0.893	0.877	0.870	0.862	0.847	0.833	0.800	0.769	0.741	0.714	0.690	0.667
2	0.961	0.925	0.890	0.857	0.826	0.797	0.769	0.756	0.743	0.718	0.694	0.640	0.592	0.549	0.510	0.476	0.444
3	0.942	0.889	0.840	0.794	0.751	0.712	0.675	0.658	0.641	0.609	0.579	0.512	0.455	0.406	0.364	0.328	0.296
4	0.924	0.855	0.792	0.735	0.683	0.636	0.592	0.572	0.552	0.516	0.482	0.410	0.350	0.301	0.260	0.226	0.198
5	0.906	0.822	0.747	0.681	0.621	0.567	0.519	0.497	0.476	0.437	0.402	0.328	0.269	0.223	0.186	0.156	0.132
6	0.888	0.790	0.705	0.630	0.564	0.507	0.456	0.432	0.410	0.370	0.335	0.262	0.207	0.165	0.133	0.108	0.088
7	0.871	0.760	0.665	0.683	0.513	0.452	0.400	0.376	0.354	0.314	0.279	0.210	0.159	0.122	0.095	0.074	0.059
8	0.853	0.731	0.627	0.540	0.467	0.404	0.351	0.327	0.305	0.266	0.233	0.168	0.123	0.091	0.068	0.051	0.039
9	0.837	0.703	0.592	0.500	0.424	0.361	0.308	0.284	0.263	0.225	0.194	0.134	0.094	0.067	0.048	0.035	0.026
10	0.820	0.676	0.558	0.463	0.386	0.322	0.270	0.247	0.227	0.191	0.162	0.107	0.073	0.050	0.035	0.024	0.017
11	0.804	0.650	0.527	0.429	0.350	0.287	0.237	0.215	0.195	0.162	0.135	0.086	0.056	0.037	0.025	0.017	0.012
12	0.788	0.625	0.497	0.397	0.319	0.257	0.208	0.187	0.168	0.137	0.112	0.069	0.043	0.027	0.018	0.012	0.008
13	0.773	0.601	0.469	0.368	0.290	0.229	0.182	0.163	0.145	0.116	0.093	0.055	0.033	0.020	0.013	0.008	0.005
14	0.758	0.577	0.442	0.340	0.263	0.205	0.160	0.141	0.125	0.099	0.078	0.044	0.025	0.015	0.009	0.006	0.003
15	0.743	0.555	0.417	0.315	0.239	0.183	0.140	0.123	0.108	0.084	0.065	0.035	0.020	0.011	0.006	0.004	0.002
16	0.728	0.534	0.394	0.292	0.218	0.163	0.123	0.107	0.093	0.071	0.054	0.028	0.015	0.008	0.005	0.003	0.002
17	0.714	0.513	0.371	0.270	0.198	0.146	0.108	0.093	0.080	0.060	0.045	0.023	0.012	0.006	0.003	0.002	0.001
18	0.700	0.494	0.350	0.250	0.180	0.130	0.095	0.081	0.069	0.051	0.038	0.018	0.009	0.005	0.002	0.001	0.001
19	0.686	0.475	0.331	0.232	0.164	0.116	0.083	0.070	0.060	0.043	0.031	0.014	0.007	0.003	0.002	0.001	0.001
20	0.673	0.456	0.312	0.215	0.149	0.104	0.073	0.061	0.051	0.037	0.026	0.012	0.005	0.002	0.001	0.001	
21	0.660	0.439	0.294	0.199	0.135	0.093	0.064	0.053	0.044	0.031	0.022	0.009	0.004	0.002	0.001		
22	0.647	0.422	0.278	0.184	0.123	0.083	0.056	0.046	0.038	0.026	0.018	0.007	0.003	0.001	0.001		
23	0.634	0.406	0.262	0.170	0.112	0.074	0.049	0.040	0.033	0.022	0.015	0.006	0.002	0.001			
24	0.622	0.390	0.247	0.158	0.102	0.066	0.043	0.035	0.028	0.019	0.013	0.005	0.002	0.001			
25	0.610	0.375	0.233	0.146	0.092	0.059	0.038	0.030	0.024	0.016	0.010	0.004	0.001	0.001			
30	0.552	0.308	0.174	0.099	0.057	0.033	0.020	0.015	0.012	0.007	0.004	0.001					
40	0.453	0.208	0.097	0.046	0.022	0.011	0.005	0.004	0.003	0.001	0.001						
50	0.372	0.141	0.054	0.021	0.009	0.003	0.001	0.001	0.001								

Note: Calculations are based on end-of-period compounding.

Table 2 PRESENT VALUE OF $1 RECEIVED ANNUALLY

Duration of Payments	2%	4%	6%	8%	10%	12%	14%	15%	16%	18%	20%	25%	30%	35%	40%	45%	50%
1	0.980	0.962	0.943	0.926	0.909	0.893	0.877	0.870	0.862	0.847	0.833	0.800	0.769	0.741	0.714	0.690	0.667
2	1.942	1.886	1.833	1.783	1.736	1.690	1.647	1.626	1.605	1.566	1.528	1.440	1.361	1.289	1.224	1.165	1.111
3	2.884	2.775	2.673	2.577	2.487	2.402	2.322	2.283	2.246	2.174	2.106	1.952	1.816	1.696	1.589	1.493	1.407
4	3.808	3.630	3.465	3.312	3.170	3.037	2.914	2.855	2.798	2.690	2.589	2.362	2.166	1.997	1.849	1.720	1.605
5	4.713	4.452	4.212	3.993	3.791	3.605	3.433	3.352	3.274	3.127	2.991	2.689	2.436	2.220	2.035	1.876	1.737
6	5.601	5.242	4.917	4.623	4.355	4.111	3.889	3.784	3.685	3.498	3.326	2.951	2.643	2.385	2.168	1.983	1.824
7	6.472	6.002	5.582	5.206	4.868	4.564	4.288	4.160	4.039	3.812	3.605	3.161	2.802	2.508	2.263	2.057	1.883
8	7.325	6.733	6.210	5.747	5.335	4.968	4.639	4.487	4.344	4.078	3.837	3.329	2.925	2.598	2.331	2.108	1.922
9	8.162	7.435	6.802	6.247	5.759	5.328	4.946	4.772	4.607	4.303	4.031	3.463	3.019	2.665	2.379	2.144	1.948
10	8.983	8.111	7.360	6.710	6.145	5.650	5.216	5.019	4.833	4.494	4.192	3.571	3.092	2.715	2.414	2.168	1.965
11	9.787	8.760	7.887	7.139	6.495	5.937	5.453	5.234	5.029	4.656	4.327	3.656	3.147	2.752	2.438	2.185	1.977
12	10.575	9.385	8.384	7.536	6.814	6.194	5.660	5.421	5.197	4.793	4.439	3.725	3.190	2.779	2.456	2.196	1.985
13	11.343	9.986	8.853	7.904	7.103	6.424	5.842	5.583	5.342	4.910	4.533	3.780	3.223	2.799	2.468	2.204	1.990
14	12.106	10.563	9.295	8.244	7.367	6.628	6.002	5.724	5.468	5.008	4.611	3.824	3.249	2.814	2.477	2.210	1.993
15	12.849	11.118	9.712	8.559	7.606	6.811	6.142	5.847	5.575	5.092	4.675	3.859	3.268	2.825	2.484	2.214	1.995
16	13.578	11.652	10.106	8.851	7.824	6.974	6.265	5.954	5.669	5.162	4.730	3.887	3.283	2.834	2.489	2.216	1.997
17	14.292	12.166	10.477	9.122	8.022	7.120	6.373	6.047	5.749	5.222	4.775	3.910	3.295	2.840	2.492	2.218	1.998
18	14.992	12.659	10.828	9.372	8.201	7.250	6.467	6.128	5.818	5.273	4.812	3.928	3.304	2.844	2.494	2.219	1.999
19	15.678	13.134	11.158	9.604	8.365	7.366	6.550	6.198	5.877	5.316	4.844	3.942	3.311	2.848	2.496	2.220	1.999
20	16.351	13.590	11.470	9.818	8.514	7.469	6.623	6.259	5.929	5.353	4.870	3.954	3.316	2.850	2.497	2.221	1.999
21	17.011	14.029	11.764	10.017	8.649	7.562	6.687	6.312	5.973	5.384	4.891	3.963	3.320	2.852	2.498	2.221	2.000
22	17.658	14.451	12.042	10.201	8.772	7.645	6.743	6.359	6.011	5.410	4.909	3.970	3.323	2.853	2.498	2.222	2.000
23	18.292	14.857	12.303	10.371	8.883	7.718	6.792	6.399	6.044	5.432	4.925	3.976	3.325	2.854	2.499	2.222	2.000
24	18.914	15.247	12.550	10.529	8.985	7.784	6.835	6.434	6.073	5.451	4.937	3.981	3.327	2.855	2.499	2.222	2.000
25	19.523	15.622	12.783	10.675	9.077	7.843	6.873	6.464	6.097	5.467	4.948	3.985	3.329	2.856	2.499	2.222	2.000
30	22.396	17.292	13.765	11.258	9.427	8.055	7.003	6.566	6.177	5.517	4.979	3.995	3.332	2.857	2.500	2.222	2.000
40	27.355	19.793	15.046	11.925	9.779	8.244	7.105	6.642	6.234	5.548	4.997	3.999	3.333	2.857	2.500	2.222	2.000
50	31.424	21.482	15.762	12.234	9.915	8.304	7.133	6.661	6.246	5.554	4.999	4.000	3.333	2.857	2.500	2.222	2.000

Note: Calculations are based on end-of-period compounding.

Table 3 CAPITAL RECOVERY FACTORS

Years to Recovery	2%	4%	6%	8%	10%	12%	14%	15%	16%	18%	20%	25%	30%	35%	40%	45%	50%
1	1.020	1.040	1.060	1.080	1.100	1.120	1.140	1.150	1.160	1.180	1.200	1.250	1.300	1.350	1.400	1.450	1.500
2	0.515	0.530	0.545	0.561	0.576	0.592	0.607	0.615	0.623	0.639	0.655	0.694	0.735	0.776	0.817	0.858	0.900
3	0.347	0.360	0.374	0.388	0.402	0.416	0.431	0.438	0.445	0.460	0.475	0.512	0.551	0.590	0.629	0.670	0.711
4	0.263	0.275	0.289	0.302	0.315	0.329	0.343	0.350	0.357	0.372	0.386	0.423	0.462	0.501	0.541	0.582	0.623
5	0.212	0.225	0.237	0.250	0.264	0.277	0.291	0.298	0.305	0.320	0.334	0.372	0.411	0.450	0.491	0.533	0.576
6	0.179	0.191	0.203	0.216	0.230	0.243	0.257	0.264	0.271	0.286	0.301	0.339	0.378	0.419	0.461	0.504	0.548
7	0.155	0.167	0.179	0.192	0.205	0.219	0.233	0.240	0.248	0.262	0.277	0.316	0.357	0.399	0.442	0.486	0.531
8	0.137	0.149	0.161	0.174	0.187	0.201	0.216	0.223	0.230	0.245	0.261	0.300	0.342	0.385	0.429	0.474	0.520
9	0.123	0.134	0.147	0.160	0.174	0.188	0.202	0.210	0.217	0.232	0.248	0.289	0.331	0.375	0.420	0.466	0.513
10	0.111	0.123	0.136	0.149	0.163	0.177	0.192	0.199	0.207	0.223	0.239	0.280	0.323	0.368	0.414	0.461	0.509
11	0.102	0.114	0.127	0.140	0.154	0.168	0.183	0.191	0.199	0.215	0.231	0.273	0.318	0.363	0.410	0.458	0.506
12	0.095	0.107	0.119	0.133	0.147	0.161	0.177	0.184	0.192	0.209	0.225	0.268	0.313	0.360	0.407	0.455	0.504
13	0.088	0.100	0.113	0.127	0.141	0.156	0.171	0.179	0.187	0.204	0.221	0.265	0.310	0.357	0.405	0.454	0.503
14	0.083	0.095	0.108	0.121	0.136	0.151	0.167	0.175	0.183	0.200	0.217	0.262	0.308	0.355	0.404	0.452	0.502
15	0.078	0.090	0.103	0.117	0.131	0.147	0.163	0.171	0.179	0.196	0.214	0.259	0.306	0.354	0.403	0.452	0.501
16	0.074	0.086	0.099	0.113	0.128	0.143	0.160	0.168	0.176	0.194	0.211	0.257	0.305	0.353	0.402	0.451	0.501
17	0.070	0.082	0.095	0.110	0.125	0.140	0.157	0.165	0.174	0.191	0.209	0.256	0.304	0.352	0.401	0.451	0.501
18	0.067	0.079	0.092	0.107	0.122	0.138	0.155	0.163	0.172	0.190	0.208	0.255	0.303	0.352	0.401	0.451	0.500
19	0.064	0.076	0.090	0.104	0.120	0.136	0.153	0.161	0.170	0.188	0.206	0.254	0.302	0.351	0.401	0.450	0.500
20	0.061	0.074	0.087	0.102	0.117	0.134	0.151	0.160	0.169	0.187	0.205	0.253	0.302	0.351	0.400	0.450	0.500
21	0.059	0.071	0.085	0.100	0.116	0.132	0.150	0.158	0.167	0.186	0.204	0.252	0.301	0.351	0.400	0.450	0.500
22	0.057	0.069	0.083	0.098	0.114	0.131	0.148	0.157	0.166	0.185	0.204	0.252	0.301	0.350	0.400	0.450	0.500
23	0.055	0.067	0.081	0.096	0.113	0.130	0.147	0.156	0.165	0.184	0.203	0.251	0.301	0.350	0.400	0.450	0.500
24	0.053	0.066	0.080	0.095	0.111	0.128	0.146	0.155	0.165	0.183	0.203	0.251	0.301	0.350	0.400	0.450	0.500
25	0.051	0.064	0.078	0.094	0.110	0.127	0.145	0.155	0.164	0.183	0.202	0.251	0.300	0.350	0.400	0.450	0.500
30	0.045	0.058	0.073	0.089	0.106	0.124	0.143	0.152	0.162	0.181	0.201	0.250	0.300	0.350	0.400	0.450	0.500
40	0.037	0.051	0.066	0.084	0.102	0.121	0.141	0.151	0.160	0.180	0.200	0.250	0.300	0.350	0.400	0.450	0.500
50	0.032	0.047	0.063	0.082	0.101	0.120	0.140	0.150	0.160	0.180	0.200	0.250	0.300	0.350	0.400	0.450	0.500

Note: Calculated as the inverse of corresponding elements in Appendix A, Table 2.

Index

Absolute profitability, 32
Annual cost, *see* Equivalent annual cost
Annual ordering costs, marginal analysis, 18-19
Annual output rate, 37
Asset stocks (levels), 4
Attainable production possibilities, 26, 28-30, 34-35
   nonlinear, 43
Average costs, marginal analysis, 11-12
Average outcome, 84
Average units held, 20

Balance sheets, 3-7
   as source of information, 3-4
Bentham, Jeremy, 2
Budget constraints (limitations), 60-63
   for future and current periods, 63

Capacity costs, 16
Capital, cost (CC), 57, 63-67, 69, 100
   marginal analysis, 11, 14
   rule of thumb on, 67
Capital budgeting, 47-68, 100
   basic rule for, 60
   function, 47
   less satifactory criteria for, 52-60
   two complications in, 60-63
Capital gains, 65-67

Capital recovery charges, defined, 56
Capital recovery factors, 56-57
   defined, 56
Carrying costs, inventory, 17-18
Cash flows, 54, 64
   present value, 50, 52
   see also Net cash flows; Operating cash flow
Certainty equivalence, 73-83, 86-91, 93-94, 100
   role of probability in, 73, 75-76, 83, 87, 90-91, 93
Complementary chance, 90
Conditional outcome, 84
Conditional payments, 92-93
Conglomerate corporations, formation, 67
Consistency, 88, 94
   logical, 83
Constant returns, 38
Corner solutions, 32, 43

Decision trees, 70-72, 74-83, 86-87
   advantages, 72
   "rolling back," 76-83, 87, 100
   strategic use, 95-96, 98, 100
Decomposability (decomposition), 89-90, 93-94
Design evaluation, 54
Direct assessment, 83, 86, 88, 100
   inconsistent, 94

111

Discounted present value, *see* Present values
Discount rates, capital budgeting, 58, 63, 66-67
Dissimilar gambles, 92
Distribution of possible outcomes, 96-100
Dividend payments, reinvestment, 64-67

Economic lives, 56-57
Electric utility pricing problem, 13-17, 101
Entire equivalence, 93-94
Equal capacity curves, 29-32
Equal profit curves, 27-32, 39-40
 defined, 27
 nonlinear, 43
Equalization of margins, 10-11
Equivalence:
 certainty, *see* Certainty equivalence in value, 92-93
Equivalent allocation and resource problems, 39, 41
Equivalent annual cost, 54-58, 100
 annual total cost, 54, 56
 lowest, 54, 56-57
Equivalent certain payments, 91
Equivalent decision diagrams, 74, 80, 82, 87
Equivalent reference gambles, 91
Exact reproduction, 49
Exact value, 95
Expected returns, 86
Expected values, 82-91, 94-95
 calculation, 84-85
 defined, 84
 monetary value, 86-87
 of zero, 89

Fixed cost (purchase cost), marginal analysis, 17-18, 20-21
Fixed-plant investment, 14
Forks, decision, 70, 80-81
 terminal, 72, 74-75, 81, 95-96
Franklin, Benjamin, 68
Freezing function, 3
Frequency distributions, 98-100
Full costs, 13

Funds flow analyses (sources and uses statements):
 absence, 4
 as source of information, 6-7
Funds sources and uses budgeting, 63-67
 shareholders' expectations in, 64-67

Game theory, 103
Government regulation, 102
 marginal analysis, 13-17
Growth stocks, 67

Holding costs, marginal analysis, 18-21

Income statements, 5-7, 9
 as source of information, 5-6
Inflationary influence, 67
Initial cost criterion, 52, 57
Integer programming methods, 45
Integer solutions, 45-46
Interest rate (rate of return), capital budgeting, 47-49, 51, 53, 55, 57-60, 63-67
Internal rate of return, 58-60
 defined, 58
Inventory lot size problem:
 increase and reduction in, 20
 marginal analysis, 17-22
Investment lives, 57
Item-by-item assessments, 83-84, 88

"Jones, Norman L.," 69-90, 94-100
 serious alternatives, 71-82, 96-98

Leveraging, defined, 66
Liability levels (stocks), 4
Linear equations, defined, 27

INDEX

Linear inequalities, defined, 27
Linear programming, 25-36, 41-44
  basic theorem, 32
  operational flexibility, 38, 41-42
Linear programming problems, 34, 36, 38, 43
  defined, 27
  two-dimensional, 41
Linear restrictions, 27, 41-43; *see also* Non-negativity restrictions; Programming constraints
Local optimum, 10
Lorie, J., 60-63

Man-machine interaction, 103
Managerial function, 1-8, 101
  basic financial data for, 3-7
Managerial goals (objectives), 2-3, 8
Marginal additions, 9-11
Marginal analysis, 9-22
  basic concepts, 9-11, 22
  of total cost (TC), 14, 16, 18
Marginal costs, 9-13
  full costs vs., 13
Marginal curves, 11-13, 16-17
Marginal losses, 9
Marginal profit, defined, 10
Marginal revenue productivity, 23, 34-36
Marginal revenues, 9-11
  capital budgeting, 51
  measurement, 13
Marginal tradeoffs, 10-11
  mathematical programming, 24, 28, 40
Marginal value, 34
Mathematical programming, 23-46, 62-63
  optimization (minimization, maximization) function, 23-26, 29, 31-32, 34-35, 40-41, 43-45
  process formulations, 36-41
Mathematical programming problems, defined, 27
Monopoly, 102-3
  natural, 14
Multiple markets, marginal analysis, 13-17
Multiple period planning, 45n, 60-63
  defined, 60
  under uncertainty, 100

Negative present value, 53
Net cash flows, 50, 82-83
  time phasing, 68
Net present value, 50-53, 58-63, 72, 98, 101
  over and above capital costs, 51
  per dollar of initial cost, 51
  prerequisite for calculating, 63
  time dimension in, 68
Net worth, 4, 100
Nonlinear returns, 103
  mathematical programming, 42-45
Non-negativity restrictions, 27, 29-30, 38, 43
  absence, 32
  nonlinear, 43-44

Objective functions, 26-27, 42-43
  defined, 26
Oil, wildcatting for, 69-90, 95-100
  as a gamble, 73-90, 96, 98, 100
Oligopoly, *see* Monopoly
Operating cash flow, 100
  mathematical programming, 34, 36
  source of information on, 5
Operating costs (expenses), 69
  marginal analysis, 14
Operating profit margins, constant, 25, 42
Operations research approach, *see* Mathematical programming
Opportunity costs, 23
  capital budgeting, 60, 62-65
Opportunity set (production possibilities frontier), 32-33
Optimal balance, 11, 20
Order quantity, marginal analysis of, 19-20
Ordering costs, marginal analysis of, 18-20
Overhead, 11

Payback period (payoff period), 52-54
  defined, 52
  timing of payments within, 52-54

Payoffs, 77, 83
    monetary, 70
    symmetric, 89
Peaking phenomenon, 13-17
Present costs, capital budgeting of, 50-51, 55
Present values, 47-53, 56-63, 100-1
    net, *see* Net present value of sequential returns, 49
    sum of, 49
    transformation of, 56
Price and output decisions, marginal analysis, 11-13
Price discrimination, marginal analysis, 13-17
Probability assessments, 84-86, 90-98
    strategic use, 95-98
    from terminal reference gambles, 94-95
Product mix (process mix), mathematical programming, 36, 39-40, 44
Production possibilities frontier, 32-33
Production possibility curve, 30-31
Production process, defined, 36-37
Production process rays, 37-40
Profit maximization goal, 2, 8, 101-2
    dispute over, 101
Profitability index, 61-62
Programming, *see* Mathematical programming
Programming constraints, 32-33, 43-44; *see also* Non-negativity restrictions

Quadriatic programming, 42-43
Qualification emphasis, 24

Rate of return, *see* Interest rate
Ratio analyses, 7-8
Reference consequences, 90
Reference gambles, 90-96
    logically identical, 94
    pairs, 93-94
Relative costs, linear programming, 31-32
Relative rankings, 56
Residual claims, 102

Resource allocation problem, 25
Resource costs, linear programming, 31-32
Resource limitations, change in, 34
Risk measurement, 66-67
Risk preference, 83-84, 88-96
    role of probability in, 90-93
    strategic use, 98-100
Risk reduction objective, 54

Safety margins, 21-22
Savage, Leonard J., 60-63, 83n
Segment slopes, constant, 32
Seismic testing, 72, 75-76, 78-81, 89n
    described, 69-70
    preference for, 87-88
    strategy based on, 98
Sensitivity analyses, 103
Shadow prices, 39-40, 62
    derivation, 34-36
Simulation, 100, 102-3
Sources and uses statements, *see* Funds flow analyses
Strategies, 70, 95-100
    complete, 96
    developmental, 103
Symmetrical outcomes (solutions), 35, 89
System models (simulation), 100, 102-3
System-wide effects, 103

Terminal acts (events), 71-75, 79, 81-82
Terminal reference gambles, 94-96
Terminal values, 74, 76-83, 95-96
    equivalent, 81-82
Total cost (TC), 14, 16, 18
    annual equivalent, 54, 56
Total resource needs, mathematical programming, 37
Total value, mathematical programming, 35-36
Tracking-trends function, 7
Tradeoffs, 103-4
    marginal, *see* Marginal tradeoffs
    mathematical programming, 30-31, 36
Transaction costs, marginal analysis, 18, 20-21

INDEX

Transitivity, 89
True costs, influences on, 67

Uncertainty, 50, 68-100, 103
  absence, 52, 54
  need to analyze, 68
  role of intuition in, 68, 73, 77, 83-84, 99

Uncertainty (*continued*)
  single period context, 99-100
  time sequence in, 95
Unit factor intensities, 37
Unit holding costs, marginal analysis, 20-21

Variable cost (purchase cost), marginal analysis, 17-18